Copyright 2020 by Stephen Wylie

First published in Great Britain in 2020 by Stephen Wylie

Paperback edition published in 2020

All rights reserved. No part of this publication may be reproduced, stored in a retrieval system, or transmitted, in any form or by any means without the prior permission of the publisher, nor be otherwise circulated in any form of binding or cover other than that in which it is published and without similar condition being imposed on the subsequent purchaser.

Cover designed by Stephen Wylie with some technical help from Michael Robinson. Front and back photographs taken and edited by Stephen Wylie at The Rescue Place, Northumberland.

ISBN: 978-1-71657-742-0

SHAK was formed in June 2006 by Stephen Wylie after the sudden death of his beloved German Shepherd cross, Shak, from Lymphoma.

Uttering those fateful words 'never again' he decided he wanted to help in the world of rescue and sold his own business to concentrate on providing an alternative to the destruction which was happening in pounds all over the country.

It was whilst working in one of those pounds Stephen quickly saw there were a lot of dogs who were troubled by the life they had led before ending up discarded. As a result, they were losing their lives simply because they had nowhere else to go and give them a chance.

Rising from such horror the charity grew to provide a lifeline to so many wonderful dogs. Only taking in abused, neglected and abandoned souls or put to sleep cases at the vets, today SHAK takes care of 60+ dogs at any one time.

By providing love, safety and sanctuary in the quiet, beautiful Northumbrian countryside just outside of Alnwick, Stephen and his team help its inhabitants to learn to trust and, as Stephen calls it, "allows them to simply be a dog again."

The charity receives no government funding or grants, all its funds are self-generated through its shops in Blyth and Amble, along with the wonderful generosity of its supporters.

It was in 2013 that Stephen wrote his first novel, It's A Dog's Life. The agonising tale of a Rottweiler being abandoned and ending up in a pound. Seen through the eyes of the dog itself, the author was able to introduce some of the characters and heart-breaking situations which he himself had encountered whilst working in rescue.

Stephen has since published two other books called 'Only Human' and 'The Castle' that deal with a man struggling with mental health issues and depression.

To see the special work Stephen and his team do, please visit www.shak.org.uk. Or if you would like to donate or help in anyway then please send an email to shak@shak.org.uk. To get your own copy of any of Stephen's other books, please visit www.stephenwylie.com.

RESCUE IN LOCKDOWN

It's the uncertainty that makes you feel so vulnerable. The not knowing how long this could last or how bad it will become. We are all on this planet for such a short time anyway, always at the Reapers disposal, but now we have the threat of a killer virus which could shorten those days even more.

We have heard of coronavirus as it has swept through other countries around the world. We have watched and waited, bracing ourselves for its arrival on our shores, like a great storm or the ice age conditions of the beast from the east.

At last the weeks of uncertainty and anticipation mean nothing. COVID-19 has arrived.

The scientists have the statistics from other countries such as Italy and of course China, the politicians have whatever sense and pattern the scientists can decipher from such a tremendous loss of life. We just have the worry and the threat to our lives.

Are there lessons to be learnt as those countries reel headfirst into mass suffering and destruction. Waiting for announcement from Prime Minister Boris Johnson tonight, they both seem a million miles away from here.

coronavirus

[k*uh*-**roh**-n*uh*-vahy-r*uh* s]

noun, plural **co·ro·na·vi·rus·es.**
any of various RNA-containing spherical viruses of the family Coronaviridae, including several that cause acute respiratory illnesses.

"Good Evening,

The coronavirus is the biggest threat this country has faced for decades – and this country is not alone.

All over the world we are seeing the devastating impact of this invisible killer.

And so tonight I want to update you on the latest steps we are taking to fight the disease and what you can do to help.

And I want to begin by reminding you why the UK has been taking the approach that we have.

Without a huge national effort to halt the growth of this virus, there will come a moment when no health service in the world could possibly cope; because there won't be enough ventilators, enough intensive care beds, enough doctors and nurses.

And as we have seen elsewhere, in other countries that also have fantastic health care systems, that is the moment of real danger.

To put it simply, if too many people become seriously unwell at one time, the NHS will be unable to handle it - meaning more people are likely to die, not just from Coronavirus but from other illnesses as well.

So, it's vital to slow the spread of the disease.

Because that is the way we reduce the number of people needing hospital treatment at any one time, so we can protect the NHS's ability to cope - and save more lives.

And that's why we have been asking people to stay at home during this pandemic.

And though huge numbers are complying - and I thank you all - the time has now come for us all to do more.

From this evening I must give the British people a very simple instruction - you must stay at home.

Because the critical thing we must do is stop the disease spreading between households.

That is why people will only be allowed to leave their home for the following very limited purposes:

- *shopping for basic necessities, as infrequently as possible*
- *one form of exercise a day - for example a run, walk, or cycle - alone or with members of your household;*
- *any medical need, to provide care or to help a vulnerable person; and*
- *travelling to and from work, but only where this is absolutely necessary and cannot be done from home.*

That's all - these are the only reasons you should leave your home.

You should not be meeting friends. If your friends ask you to meet, you should say No.

You should not be meeting family members who do not live in your home.

You should not be going shopping except for essentials like food and medicine - and you should do this as little as you can. And use food delivery services where you can.

If you don't follow the rules the police will have the powers to enforce them, including through fines and dispersing gatherings.

To ensure compliance with the Government's instruction to stay at home, we will immediately:

- *close all shops selling non-essential goods, including clothing and electronic stores and other premises including libraries, playgrounds and outdoor gyms, and places of worship;*
- *we will stop all gatherings of more than two people in public – excluding people you live with;*
- *and we'll stop all social events, including weddings, baptisms and other ceremonies, but excluding funerals.*

Parks will remain open for exercise but gatherings will be dispersed.

No Prime Minister wants to enact measures like this.

I know the damage that this disruption is doing and will do to people's lives, to their businesses and to their jobs.

And that's why we have produced a huge and unprecedented programme of support both for workers and for business.

And I can assure you that we will keep these restrictions under constant review. We will look again in three weeks, and relax them if the evidence shows we are able to.

But at present there are just no easy options. The way ahead is hard, and it is still true that many lives will sadly be lost.

And yet it is also true that there is a clear way through.

Day by day we are strengthening our amazing NHS with 7500 former clinicians now coming back to the service.

With the time you buy - by simply staying at home - we are increasing our stocks of equipment.

We are accelerating our search for treatments.

We are pioneering work on a vaccine.

And we are buying millions of testing kits that will enable us to turn the tide on this invisible killer.

I want to thank everyone who is working flat out to beat the virus.

Everyone from the supermarket staff to the transport workers to the carers to the nurses and doctors on the frontline.

But in this fight we can be in no doubt that each and every one of us is directly enlisted.

Each and every one of us is now obliged to join together.

To halt the spread of this disease.

To protect our NHS and to save many many thousands of lives.

And I know that as they have in the past so many times.

The people of this country will rise to that challenge.

And we will come through it stronger than ever.

We will beat the coronavirus and we will beat it together.

And therefore, I urge you at this moment of national emergency to stay at home, protect our NHS and save lives.

Thank you"

Boris Johnson. Prime Minister of the United Kingdom.

23.03.2020

Lockdown

The Prime Minister's speech said it all. We have to stay off the streets, we have to stay apart, we have to self-isolate.

It's just after nine pm on Monday the 23rd of March 2020, I am sitting in my old Louis style chair and I have just watched history in the making.

My mind goes into overdrive, I become confused, I feel the worry of everybody else, I feel under pressure to make a decision.

We have a dedicated team of volunteers, which complement the work myself and my staff do, all of whom work or have commitments elsewhere. They all have families to protect and people who depend on them, but there are also our dogs.

Which is why I am torn.

At the kennels we have maybe half a dozen dogs which are only handled by either myself or my deputy Rich. Intricate souls who have so many stories to tell. Stories which mean the dogs are so damaged not only are we the only ones who can take them out on walks, we are also the only ones who can safely get into their kennels. Without either of us their world becomes a very small and lonely place.

Lockdown. Stay at home.

Those words ring around my head like the siren of a Police car speeding to attend to some disaster in somebody else's world. Passing me by but dragging me into the confusion and terror of what is happening. A witness to the accident, only viewed from a far.

Social distancing, allowed out to exercise once a day, keep away from anyone which you don't share your home with, stay indoors. We are all doomed.

The thoughts which go through my head make me feel nauseous, that deep and uncomfortable sensation which surges through my body, riddling my veins with nervous tingles. Overpowering like the smell of onions being chopped, the tingles effect my mind and my movements. I sit there, in the old chair, shell shocked and unable to stand.

My girlfriend, Rachel, had joined me halfway through the speech. Neither of us spoke, we just sat and listened. I look at her now and see in her eyes she is experiencing the exact same damned tingles that I am. The fear and apprehension etched across her face like some sort of fairground face painting. The feeling of being trapped, she has to get home to her daughter at some point.

We hold each other close but say nothing. An embrace born out hopelessness and dismay. We move apart and still say nothing, instead we both just stare at the screen of the Samsung mobile phone which has just shattered our worlds, maybe forever.

"We'll get through this." Rachel says, breaking the silence at last. I nod without replying. I really can't see how.

Money

At the kennels we have five members of staff, two full time and three part time. The current situation has already led to the temporary closure of our SHAK Shop on Saturday. Nobody had been in for days, our main source of income for wages was gone. Cut off like flicking the light switch. All the work which had gone into establishing the shop by a complete voluntary workforce, was now left completely in the dark. We have no idea when we will be allowed to turn the lights back on.

What little money we have in the bank will soon be gone, within a matter of weeks, with no viable way of us making any more for the foreseeable future.

I'd seen this coming, the inevitable big black cloud looming down, sneering at us as it slowly makes its way over the hill tops, making its way from China, its deep, dark shadow polluting the usual view of green fields and trees.

Trying to hold the storm back as much as I could, five days before Boris Johnson's announcement we were all prisoners in a society which was beginning to die, I launched an online appeal begging people for funds. Without having some sort of contingency plan to replace the shop takings, we would have to lose our team of staff and all the experience which they bring. We wouldn't have the people to walk the dogs and clean. I would be the only person who could handle the difficult dogs, everything would be over.

Yes, we could place some of the dogs with other rescues if there was room, but for many the only alternative would be the very action they had avoided already by being brought to us, the vet's needle.

To take their lives like that would be against everything I believe in. It would be failure and disgusting. I would be no better than the people who had let them down so badly prior to them making their way into my life and the lives of the SHAK family.

Everything we have achieved over the last fourteen years would amount to nothing. We would be no better than anybody else. I don't think I could live with myself if it comes to that.

Death is final.

So, on Thursday the 19th March 2020 I had to roll the last dice, play the master card, declare to the world, which was already in turmoil, we too were struggling to survive.

"It's with a very heavy heart I have to type this message, but developments of the last 48 hours or so has plunged the whole charity into crisis leaving everything we have ever worked for in serious jeopardy.

Since the outbreak of the Corona virus the takings in the shop have plummeted. The town is empty and it's a trend that's getting worse. On top of that, the government's Self Isolating for the Over 70's scheme has severely affected the retail workforce, including the management that runs it.

We are left with no option to announce that the shop will close at the end of business this Saturday.

We are in negotiations to try and get a crew of staff to cover maybe a Friday and Saturday, but obviously even if we can do this it will be just until if or when the government close the retail sector down.

It's not just financially we will lose out, although there will be more on that later, obviously the majority of our bedding and food donations come through the shop door. Without either we then have another serious issue.

A sudden change in circumstances means our online sales is currently limited, although we are trying to get as much sold via Ebay as we can.

All in all, it means that we somehow need to raise between £1,000 and £1,300 per WEEK just to operate as we are now, until normality resumes. That is how much this is all affecting us.

The alternative is that all staff are made redundant and I run the place on my own with voluntary help when it's available. Whilst I am trying to make myself believe that would be possible, 7 days and 356 days a year it is most certainly not. Plus, the loss of a greatly experienced workforce would have such a detrimental effect on what we could give to the dogs.

There is of course also the worry of the virus itself. Everybody has to stay safe. And we have the concern of if anybody comes down with symptoms our entire workforce could be wiped out.

That would basically leave us with no option but to close. I don't need to spell out the position that would leave a lot of our dogs in.

I don't know where we go from here, other than to launch one last desperate appeal to save the whole organisation. I know so many other small charities are in the same position, but I have to give it my all. I couldn't live knowing our dogs had died because of this.

If you can spare anything at such a desperate time, you can by PayPal: paypal.me/shaksanctuary

Or by posting a cheque made payable to SHAK to SHAK HQ, Greenwell Road, Alnwick NE66 1HB"

The appeal has gotten off to an amazing start, the support from people who appreciate all we do has quite honestly blown me away, we are so lucky to have such fabulous support.

Striking early will hopefully be advantageous, but with the uncertainty which has swirled around like dead leaves in a courtyard for what seems like forever, and now the fact that the entire UK has entered lockdown. we have no idea how long this will all go on. How long will it be before people's money and supplies run out? How long will the dog food we have stored away, be enough to feed the 59 dogs which we are currently responsible for? What happens if the damned disease makes its way to one of us?

Day One, First Day Of Lockdown.

Tuesday 24th March 2020

Total UK Deaths: 89 deaths reported today alone. Nationwide total 424.

The number of confirmed COVID-19 cases in UK: 8,077

- The number of deaths and new cases in the UK is gathering pace, despite it feeling like you are living in a real life horror film, people are dying. More will, of that everybody seems in agreement. Today the figures across the rest of the world are also rising and give a clear indication of where we are heading unless people take precautions and follow the PM's instructions to self-isolate. In France the number of people who have died up to today is 1100, a rise of 240 in 24 hours. Italy, it's even worse, there has been 743 deaths in the same 24 hour period taking the total to 6,820. More than 69,000 people in the country have tested positive.

(Figures from Sky News)

The figures above are why we must take this all so seriously. They are why, sitting in my antique chair which has probably outlived so many people taken by this disease, I decided I had to take severe action last night. I knew people would be upset, I was expecting the protests and the confrontation. I knew people would be hurt, but I had to protect our dogs by making sure we could still function. After all, survival is the most important thing in my responsibility as the chairman and founder of SHAK.

    Sitting with Rachel holding my hand, supporting me even though her initial reaction was to take more time to think about it, I followed Boris Johnson's lead and put the entire world of SHAK in complete lockdown.

I hatched a plan in my head which seemed simple, but still there was a worry I could get a phone call at any point to say somebody was ill, or somebody they had been in contact with was. Two teams were formed, splitting the five staff members and me to make groups of three. I decided the best way to avoid contamination would be a shift pattern of three days on and three days off. However, that in itself provide a couple of major stumbling points.

In our ranks we have two full time employees, which means they work five days per week. The three day rota meant there wasn't enough work to shifts to complete their hours. Secondly, we have two members of staff who work part time, and less than three days per week. We couldn't possibly commit to paying overtime in the present situation, we were losing far too much money already.

Only one member of staff was unaffected, she was contracted to work three days per week anyway. My heart sank at the very thought of having to ask for more, but my head assured me it was the only way to go forward safely.

I will admit I was a little nervous asking two members of staff to drop two days per week, whilst the thought of asking two more to up their shifts for no financial reward was as equally daunting.

Working with our dogs is something very special. You see some horrendous things, the result of years of neglect or abuse, but you also see some amazing recoveries. The never say die attitude my staff display on a daily basis would have to face it's biggest test yet in this dreadful time, the results of what we have already achieved left me hopeful this would be another happy ending. It was now the charity's turn to be saved. I sent out messages and waited.

Hours cut and shifts increased on a voluntary basis for the three weeks of the lockdown, without any complaints at all, we could now push forward and put all of our efforts into making sure the dogs didn't notice any disruption in service. After all, they had no idea what was going on in the outside world. Coronavirus meant nothing to them.

We are all very proud of the way we work on a daily basis. We have a system of working which gives the dogs a bit of order and perhaps more importantly a bit of routine. Fed twice and the pride of at least two walks per day, means our dogs get more than from their days than many domestic pets. After speaking to the staff, we are all determined nothing was going to change, but we usually worked with a team of six people in for the full day. Cutting to half numbers was going to be a challenge. With the staff on board, it was now back to me to come up with a plan which would make it all possible. The fear of failure compressing my brain and making my heart race.

Last summer we were lucky enough to receive several grants to transform our outdoor exercise area. Nothing more than an old silage pit, which was falling apart, and in obvious need of extensive repair. It was borderline whether it should be condemned.

As part of the work we submitted plans to build six outdoor kennels which would face into the sun all day, whilst the wall of old railway sleepers which formed the area meant wind is very minimal in there. With a roof to provide shade and shelter from both the sun and the rain, these kennels were now perfect for the changes which we were going to have to make to our daily routine.

Normally when the kennels are cleaned, the dogs go out for a short walk. Both time consuming and monotonous, putting the dogs in the new kennels would be a big help.

Letting the dogs relax and get some sun on their fur, whilst chewing on a bone substitute or devouring the inside of a Kong, gave us enough time for all three staff members to clean the kennels instead of one. This system would mean we could get the cleaning done quicker and we would have more time in the afternoon for the dogs to still enjoy their walks and even take them further perhaps.

Team A, which consisted of myself, Rachel and Collette set about trialling it the morning after the Prime Minister's orders. It was hard work, but we kept up the trend of the dogs being outdoors twice. Result.

There is a great satisfaction in knowing you have done all you can in making the daytime of our dogs lives as good as you can. We all went home exhausted, but we were all also very proud we hadn't let the dogs down. A thorough cleanse of all surfaces, door handles, light switches etc before we left meant the place was safe for our colleagues, now it was over to Team B.

Day Two.

Wednesday 25th March 2020

Total UK Deaths: 467

Confirmed Cases: 9,642

- Prince Charles is diagnosed as positive for Coronavirus.
- British Embassy Diplomat Steven Dick dies from the disease.
- Chloe Middleton aged just 21 becomes the youngest person with no pre-existing health issues to die from COVID-19.
- 405,000 people sign up to be volunteers to help the NHS.

Today is my first day self-isolating, as I begin my three days away from the kennels. The shift pattern which we had done prior to lockdown meant my team had just completed three days. Given the pressure of trialling the new system yesterday, it was agreed Team B would commence with the responsibility of three days in from today. I feel anxious at the pressure they will be under, but I have faith Rich, Sarah and Catherine will manage.

It's by far from a day off though, as I know I can't just sit outside in the gorgeous spring sunshine which seems to have appeared just when those black clouds of depression and disease have taken over the skyline of the country.

I have an abundance of paperwork to catch up on, emails to read and reply too, the list of admin jobs is endless. It is testament to my dedication which shows the dogs come first in my role in the charity, after all it was having the opportunity to spend my working life alongside these amazing animals I formed this charity in the first place. I do, however, understand I have created a monster of gigantic proportions, and with that comes a responsibility for office work.

I spend the entire morning and best part of the afternoon ploughing through bank statements and previous records as I look to complete several Gift Aid claims which have been neglected and on my mind for quite some mind. I have mixed emotions at both facing an enormous task but also at setting to clear a 'nag' from the back of my mind. I know it is one of those jobs I will be relieved is done once it is completed. Surround by paper and with the laptop staring back at me, I set off on a journey back in time.

Gift Aid is where a registered charity can claim back the tax on your donation if you're a UK Taxpayer, it works out at 25p per pound, so my days efforts are well worth it as I submit two claims worth over a combined £1750.

It's not just me 'in the office' though, my mother Joan, who manages the shop in her retirement, is in her seventies. The government has made her housebound for twelve weeks. She is going mad after five days but knows it's for her and her husband Mike's safety.

She is constantly scouring the news and Facebook for news of grants or possible donations. Volunteers Jon and Sandra are filling in the applications Joan finds, as well as using Sandra's experience as a retired accountant to produce predicted cash flow forecasts. Everybody is working so hard to try and find a way through this. It is still very early days in what will no doubt being hanging over us for a long time, but it is easy to see everyone, not just me, is so worried.

The money is still a huge weight on my mind. We are living day by day without the income from the shop, but the appeal is still going extremely well. Six days after it was launched, the total stands over £6,000.

Such a fantastic amount of money in such a short time, it shows the support for our work out there. It illustrates you all want us to succeed and how much not only our efforts are appreciated, but how much our dogs are loved for overcoming such atrocities in their lives before they found us. Never before has this support been so vital.

There is also the incredible gesture of a Porsche 911 Carrera Cabriolet donated to the charity for us to raffle off or sell.

The car every boy dreams of, now somebody has so much faith in my vision they have donated one to help saves us. We will of course need to wait for more settled times before we gain the benefit, but a little bit of me feels like a kid in a sweet shop. We have a Porsche. A Porsche 911 Carrera Cabriolet!!

Whilst all of this is beyond our wildest dreams, there is still the uncertainty of how long this will all last. If we look at the amount I mentioned in the appeal, which we are missing every week, the donations so far give us about five weeks extra to survive.

To add to the pressure our vets are now also closed because of the virus. Although they are offering telephone consults and Emily who has looked after us for so many years, has offered to help us in any way she can. It just feels like another screw tightened in the frame which could eventually crush us to death. We will fight and beat this, but it is affecting so many people, everybody in the world is in this together. Thoughts like that emphasise just how critical this is, how vulnerable we all are. We really could be living through the end of the world.

As I said earlier, Rich, Catherine and Sarah began the first shift of three days in today. I have to admit I was nervous this morning, not because I don't have complete faith in them, just because I wasn't there. I am so used to being around when times are hard, sitting here helpless, even though it made us money, feels wrong. I feel uncomfortable and lazy, helpless and like I'm letting the dogs and staff down. Then the phone bleeps with more sad news as more people are diagnosed or die. I know the plan I have brought in is for everyone's safety. I know deep down it is the right thing to be doing, but it still doesn't numb the hopelessness I feel at not being in. Despite doing so much work and getting a huge chunk of the Gift Aid completed, the tingles in the stomach are still there.

Teatime arrives along with an update. I shouldn't have been nervous. Team B have excelled today following the system we trialled yesterday, all the dogs got outside twice. Amazing work which means we have all experienced the feeling getting it done brings, and the exhaustion.

In the big outside things seem to be getting worse. Prince Charles, heir to the throne, has been diagnosed as positive for COVID-19 after testing, although reports say the symptoms are mild and he is otherwise in good health. It would seem coronavirus has no respect for sovereignty.

However, the dreadful news about Chloe Middleton should send shock waves around the world. It was thought people aged sixty or above were the ones likely to become fatally infected, unless there was some other under lying health condition. It shows we still know very little about what we are fighting against. The evil power behind this virus is the unknown. We all need to listen to the advice and stay indoors, we need to isolate, we need to stay safe.

Day Three.

Thursday 26th March 2020

Total Deaths in UK: 584

Confirmed Cases: 11,658

- Vets asked to donate ventilators to hospitals
- North Yorkshire Police to bring in road checkpoints to make sure journeys are essential.
- Spain announce 655 deaths in 24 Hours bringing their death total to 4,089.
- Half a million people worldwide have now been infected by the coronavirus.

I wake up to another sunny spring day, such a contrast to the disturbing and bleak situation the country finds itself in. Once again, I prepare myself for a day of admin and finishing off the Gift Aid claims which will bring us right up to date.

I miss the fresh air and the company of the dogs at the kennels, but know they are in good hands with Team B. I am not alone in this though; I am still receiving messages from volunteers asking when they can come back up. I know they are missing it as much as I am, but it only confirms my belief once again we are doing the right thing. As much as it hurts, I must put the dogs first. Three people may be a lot less than they are used to, but if the virus took hold in there it would wipe us out completely. Then what would we do? I just really hope it is only for original three weeks which Boris Johnson stated.

When I launched the appeal last week, I had a search through the media contacts I have acquired over the years. Most were unobtainable or no longer interested in what we do. However, one stuck out in particular who would maybe be interested in giving our plight some airtime. It was worth a shot.

I have been invited on Alfie Joey's breakfast radio show on BBC Radio Newcastle quite a few times now. Usually when something unsavoury makes headline news involving a dog, so it seemed fair to ask if he would be interested in running this story.

"Yes Stephen!! We're inundated at the moment, but we need this story on air. Please call in next week between 6-10am!! We'll take the call, put you on air and get the story out there!!"

That was of course, before we all went into lockdown. I appreciate everybody is going through all of this, we are not the only ones struggling. There are so many sad and desperate tales out there, I felt it was respectful to wait a couple of days whilst the panic hopefully subsided and people began to understand what was happening. A big factor in being successful in the media I have learnt over the years, is getting the timing right. For people to fully appreciate our plight and to put the dogs at the forefront of their minds, I needed to pick my moment. This morning was the morning.

I think the interview went well. I mentioned how much of a devasting effect the situation has had on our finances, the commitment and dedication of the staff and the sacrifices which they have all made. I mentioned the dogs were still getting the same attention every day despite everything. When asked if we would make it through this, I paused. I wanted to say we had to, I wanted to declare if we didn't dogs would die. The words just wouldn't come though, the thought of it actually happening was just too much to say it out loud. The saliva around my tongue vanished, my ears began to hear nothing but a constant chime as I stood slightly shaking trying to think of what to say.

The pause seemed to last forever, then I opened my mouth and managed to speak.

"I hope so. We plan to." Was all I could say.

Within minutes of coming off air we had received £210 in donations.

For a few years now I have written a SHAK column in the local newspaper, the Northumberland Gazette. The paper has always been incredibly supportive of our work, giving our dogs stories pages has meant the awareness in Northumberland and specifically Alnwick, plus the villages around, has grown dramatically. This in turn has been vital in us growing as a charity and becoming a 'brand' which people recognise and understand.

One of their reporters picked up on the appeal from our website a few days ago and asked if he could use it to run a story to try and get us help. The result is a half-page in today's newspaper.

I am obviously biased, but with so much else happening in the world, I really appreciate the fact not all the media has forgotten animals will suffer with this too. Their lives are at risk just as much as ours.

Day Four.

Friday 27th March 2020

Total UK Deaths: 769

Confirmed Cases: 12,324

- Boris Johnson, Prime Minister of the UK tests positive for the Coronavirus. As does Health Secretary Matt Hancock, whilst Chief Medical Officer Chris Whitty self-isolates with symptoms.
- Councils asked to house all people who sleep rough by the weekend.
- USA report 86,000 cases of COVID-19. That is more than China and Italy and 16% of the world's total of 532,000.
- Italy announce 919 deaths in one day. Death Total now: 9,134 with confirmed cases at 86,498 which is even more than China who have confirmed 81,897.
- Ireland put into lockdown.
- Birmingham Airport is to be the site of a temporary mortuary to hold up to 12,000 bodies, to accompany London's Excel Centre.

Another glorious sunny morning, I am awoken at around 6am by the sound of the new-born lambs in the fields which surround my house. Their bleats are accompanied by the majestic song of numerous different breeds of birds, all singing different words, but all joining in the same song, morning has broken.

It is nature at its most beautiful and innocent. New life and others preparing nests for the arrival of more, it is as if nobody has told mother nature of the pandemic which is swallowing the humanity it shares the earth with. Or maybe they have and she either doesn't care or thinks its what we deserve.

I wonder why this is happening, why are we all going through this. Is it to rid the world of the weak and elderly so the human race can start again? Or is it a punishment for abusing the world and taking it for our own? A gentle reminder to illustrate we are not the be all and end all, nor do we call all the shots. We are as naive and vulnerable as the lambs and birds who serenade me this morning. We are all in this together, but the animals we so often butcher could end up having the last laugh in this case. These days we are the lambs to the slaughter.

As the sunlight begins to streak across my face, I drift off into a snooze which cannot really be described as 'sleep.' Surrounded by the dogs I foster for SHAK, Donnie and Henry snoring, Haden stretched out on the bed with his head resting on my legs, I wonder if they realise something is so wrong.

Today is my last day in self isolation before I return to the kennels to do three days on. I have worked so hard with trying to publicise our plight and to raise funds, I plan to have a day outside surrounded by the nature which woke me. I live in a detached old farmhouse in the middle of nowhere. I have no neighbours other than the sheep, the birds, the deer and the owls. If I had to pick a place to live in during such a crisis, it would be very similar to here. It's like having my own little world and one which I should be safe in. There's a word for you, "safe." If we do get through this, unscathed and operating the way we were before, then we must all stay safe. I can do my bit by setting out the conditions, but at the end of the day it is down to each and every individual to look after themselves and understand.

I get out of bed and check my phone. Emails, texts and PayPal notifications. I sit back down on the edge, rubbing my eyes and taking a deep breath. I'll deal with these first.

The appeal has been incredible. Running for a week now, we have so far raised £8,702. An incredible amount and one which brings home how much people value what we do. This immediate cash input takes off a lot of pressure. We now have the money to last an extra month, but in the back of my mind is the fear of uncertainty, what if this goes on for months or years. There is no closing date for this virus, no plan set out which has an expiry date. We are all living in the unknown. The comfort of familiarity and routine has gone. Each and every person is now living in fear of illness and death being just around the corner. There is no sunlit horizon in sight for anybody to ride off into.

I know how worried I am about the charity, my family and my own personal circumstances. I cannot begin to imagine what others are going through. The over 70's who have been told to confine themselves to their homes for at least three months.

Can you possibly imagine how it must feel having walked this earth freely for so long? Can you picture the fear which such a message must instil? Panic and isolation all rolled into one package which nobody really knows how to unwrap. My own parents fit into that category, but thankfully they are both relatively fit and well. I worry about others, the disabled, the blind, the deaf and those souls with dementia. What little liberation they have has gone. It must be so frightening; how do we expect them to even comprehend what is happening never mind adjust to it.

The way I had planned to spend my day didn't quite materialise. Those messages on my phone, which I checked when I got up, turned into a full day's work.

An amazing lady who has supported me from day one, was first on the phone. She runs her own rescue., I have refrained from naming her to eliminate the risk of embarrassment. However, she had read the report in the Northumberland Gazette and was worried. This lady has always respected the work I set out to achieve, she was there for me when I realised the killing in pounds was wrong. Today she is still there for me, offering a donation of £2,000.

After her call, the phone went again. This time with a marketing representative from the Gazette, wanting to help us in any way they could. We talked, but I think we both agreed we were doing all we could for now.

Then the news broke.

Boris Johnson, the man leading this country has tested positive for COVID-19. Very quickly, the Health Secretary Matt Hancock, also confirms he is suffering from the virus. Then Chief Medical Officer Chris Whitty goes into self-isolation with symptoms.

On a day when records are broken with deaths and confirmed cases across the globe, to see the people responsible for getting us out of this are now stricken by this awful disease, makes me realise even more how vulnerable we all are. This disease is relentless. It could take any one of us if and when it wants. The sobering knowledge we have no vaccine, or no cure just magnifies the fear. Boris Johnson is the most powerful man in this country right now, yet nobody can guarantee him an easy recovery. He too must let fate decide.

In four separate conversations on the phone, I hear people saying they really can't see any way out of this within the three week lockdown period. They all feel as if this will go on for a long time, each phase of self-containment implemented in shorter, more acceptable proportions. I have the same fears myself, although externally I am trying to be positive and remain upbeat. Deep down my heart knows it won't be the case. A cure won't present itself in such a short length of time.

Ultimately, we could be in this situation, or worse, for a long time to come.

Day Five.

Saturday 28th March 2020

Total UK Deaths: 1,028 a rise of 259 (At least 13 of which had no underlying health problems.)

Confirmed Cases: 17,089

- Cabinet member Alister Jack self-isolating after displaying symptoms.

My first day back at the kennels and it was a weird feeling for several reasons. Firstly, I'm not really used to having three days off consecutively, so going in after so long away seems strange. I feel like I have neglected the dogs, which is crazy considering it has only been three days, but I can't help it, I have had too many years of not getting time away. Looking into the eyes of each and every one of them, I see they are pleased to see me, I can also see they are trying to understand the adjustments to their daily routine. They deserve so much more than this. It is our jobs to make it work so they do.

Secondly, going into no volunteers and seeing the job which lay in front of us, brought everything home to us all and quickly diminished the nostalgia at seeing all the dogs again. There is a job to be done here, a very difficult one it is too.

Team B has done a great job implementing the process we trialled on Tuesday, so despite everything all the dogs have still been outside twice every day. A fantastic achievement which shows immense dedication. It would be so easy to just do the minimum, get them fed, cleaned and then fed again. We are all feeling the pressure already, the daunting feeling of not wanting to fail, so to have worked as hard as Team B has and made it work, provides immense motivation for us.

We got through it today, with Collette and Rachel both working incredibly hard. It was non-stop, and at times I thought it may not happen but giving the dogs the nearest we possibly could to their normal routine made it all worthwhile. I know the dogs are aware something is happening, but hopefully the model we are putting in place and the system which is being implemented will have taken their minds off the fact there is less people about. At the end of the day all they really want is to be fed and walked, as long as we keep doing so, they should be happy. We are and they seem to be.

After work I popped to the local Sainsbury's to try and get something nice for tea. I never made it through the doors. People were queuing across the car park; security were making sure they were well separated from the person in front. People were being allowed into the shop in small numbers as others came out. People in the queue were wearing masks covering their mouths and noses.

I have never seen anything like this in my lifetime, and never thought I would. It was like something from an 'end of the world' film. Worrying and disturbing, the satisfaction of the day's work quickly wore off as I sat in the van looking at apocalyptic Alnwick. We really are in trouble here, big trouble. I never thought I would live through something like this in my lifetime. To see such a normal and mundane task as getting the weekly shopping being regulated like something out of a prisoner of war camp in the old movies, is both disconcerting and upsetting. I feel ashamed I am part of something like this. Ashamed and embarrassed. I still can't believe this is happening.

Tonight, at home it hasn't been great either. I am really worried about Sheba, a little German Shepherd which I foster.

She must be about fourteen and a half now, having come to me aged twelve and a half according to her microchip. She was dumped in a locked school field, which was all fenced in, early one Saturday morning. People watched her walk around all day, until she was finally caught at about 6pm. Weak on her rear legs, she could hardly stand.

She came up to our kennels and when I saw the state of her back end, I instantly made the decision to bring her home. I thought I would be lucky if I shared life with her for a week.

Once I got her settled on the first night, I asked her if she wanted to sleep downstairs or come upstairs with the rest of us. She shot past me and up the stairs faster than I had seen her move at any other time. She has spent most of her time since, stretched out next to my side of the bed.

We tracked her previous owner down but for legal reasons I cannot really go any further into it. Despite clearly abandoning her, the authorities were unable to prosecute him. Just another glaring example of the ridiculous flaws in the Animal Welfare Act.

She is lying right beside me on the floor next to the bed right now, resting her eyes. Her backend has been weak for as long as I have known her, but today it seems to have given in.

I think Sheba suffers from dementia too, she wanders around all the time, maybe she has just over done it? She is so old it wouldn't take much to leave her muscles exhausted at over exertion. A good night's rest might make all the difference, she may feel a bit stronger in the morning. I try so hard to make myself believe such a theory, but experience and instinct tell me otherwise.

She has a nice colour in her gums, with blood returning very quickly when pressed. She is alert and aware of what is going on around her, still desperate to please and to be close, but I can't help but think she has a worried look in her eyes.

Vets are closed because of the coronavirus, although they are open for telephone consults, I don't even have a visit as an option. I have already checked all the things they would ask me to over the phone.

She is asleep now; I can see her ribs breathing in and out as her dreams take her to places which I will never know. What I do know is I'm so pleased she is here, and I am lucky she found her way to me when she needed somewhere to go. I have owned German Shepherds for over twenty one years now, they are a breed which I have a great connection with, Sheba is one of the sweetest I have ever met.

    I will not let her suffer but want to see how she goes after a good night's rest. I am not opposed to using things like wheelchairs if the dog accepts it, but with her dementia and constant walking about that may not be an option. My heart tells me there is more going on inside, something dark and sinister which I won't be able to defend her from.

    I can hear her breathing now as she falls deeper into sleep. Leaning back onto my pillow so I can do the same, my hand is draped over the side of the bed, resting on her head. I love her and her quaint little ways so much.

Day Six.

Sunday 29th March 2020

Total UK Deaths: 1,235

Confirmed Cases: 19,522

- Prime Minister warns it may take "six months before normal life resumes."
- Amged El-Hawrani, an NHS consultant is the first frontline hospital worker in the UK to die of COVID-19.

There is nothing but grey this morning. No sun, no birds singing, just the odd noise of a distressed lamb looking for its mother, as it tries to understand snow for the first time.

The harsh reality as hail stones smash of the windows, remind me of what a miserable situation we are facing as soon as I open my eyes. Bleak, unforgiving and relentless, today is the first day of British Summertime.

The A1 is barren. I do not see a single vehicle on the desolate land scape until I turn off the motorway and venture along the country road to the kennels. The feeling driving into work is almost eerie. It's as if me and Rachel are the only people in the world who have somewhere to go. It feels like we are the only people in existence, the world has ended.

Passing a young deer whose life has been taken at some point during the dark that proceeded the bland dawn of the misery of today. Its frame obliterated almost beyond any form of shape, its body stretched and flattened like a shirt through a mangle, the pressure of the impact means that its head has no choice in raising and looking straight at me. It's ears upright as if they have been pinned, the driver who will eventually follow my path will see the same grim look in the eyes of the deceased.

As will the next, then the next, then the next until eventually somebody will decide to put the face of this young doe out of her misery. Her skull will take the same form as the rest of her body, flattened and nothing more than litter on the road. Something so young taken too early. It makes me think how insecure the wildlife may feel at the lack of human interference. She probably felt it was safe to cross the road because she hadn't seen any vehicles for a long time. The deer made her decision thinking she was safe, but ultimately, she was not and paid the most precious price. Sound familiar?

Sheba is cuddling into Rachel in the passenger seat. As I expected the nights rest hasn't really made much of a difference to how she is feeling. She is frightened and is struggling to comprehend what is going on, this isn't the back of the van with the rest of the dogs. I can see the look in her eyes which want me to confirm I am in control and everything will be ok. Her pupils are dilated, and she looks uncomfortable, but I do not want to put her in the back where I can't see her. A feeling deep down is telling me not to take my eyes off her ever again. I am trying to stay positive, but instinct tells me to cherish every valuable minute we are together. Today she is going to be curled up in a nice warm bed in my office.

My office. That reminds me I have so much more to do. I have a strong feeling this problem within Great Britain isn't going to be sorted out within the next two weeks. There is no way this lockdown period will be the last or be solved after the initial three weeks. This could go on for months, or even years.

We rely heavily on donated items, luckily, we do extremely well, but if this does go on for longer than the originally predicted twenty one days, we will really struggle. The generosity of our supporters supplies us with bedding, food, cleaning products. With the both our shop and the donation drop off points closed it won't take long until we have next to nothing. It is my job to make sure we don't fall into that catastrophic situation.

The appeal for funds today has broken the £10,000 mark, which is beyond our wildest dreams. This generosity will hopefully help us get through this, but then there is the issue of being able to spend it on the supplies we need. Out of worry I decide we should be stocked up with essentials just in case this does go on longer than we all hope. Panic buying? A practice which I have been against since this crisis begun. Maybe I am overreacting, we will be ok, or maybe now I am the one beginning to panic.

Amazon Prime has been an incredible discovery for me personally, but in these times when you have to que up and wear a mask just to get into a supermarket, deliveries to my door sound so appealing and will make a big difference to how we operate.
So, today I use some of the money raised in the appeal to order kennel disinfectant, bin liners, poo bags, dishwasher tablets and laundry liquid. All essential in our daily operation and available to by online. I order in bulk and more than we would normally order, for one reason and for one reason alone. The scenes outside Sainsbury's yesterday has scared me.

I feel anger and sympathy, I feel a need to shout out "we will be ok if we all help ourselves to help others." I feel we are a long way from getting to the end of this fight. I am in shock and don't fully understand. If this is Mother Nature pressing the refresh button, then so be it, but to be unable to function in a normal fashion and being able to purchase the things we all need from a shop without having to queue just to gain entry, is to me an alarm bell of enormous magnitude. The world really is beginning to end.

Instead of sounding off, as no one is around to hear anyway, I order supplies which will hopefully see us through a couple of months and mean we won't have to worry about them. Taking my frustration out by a bit of online retail therapy. How ironic.

It is another difficult day workwise, but we get it done. I scour the supplies for a wheelchair which will fit Sheba, only for the one donated flat packed and still in its box, to be too small after Rachel has spent time and built it up. Back to square one. Maybe I am clutching at straws.

I am so worried about her, but she is constantly looking for me. I don't know if it's for reassurance or out of fear. I am making sure I am there as many times as possible. Everything now revolves around her. I know she is dying. I know the world around us is dying. There is no hope and no future as things stand. All the politicians are trying to demonstrate there will be an end to all of this, but they don't really know. I am trying to talk myself and anyone who will listen into believing Sheba will get better. There must be some form of hope in both cases, but deep down in the darkest part of my heart, I fear there isn't any for either.

Just before we are about to leave, Collette notices Cooper is shaking as he lies in his kennel. He gets up and is excited when I go to his kennel door with a lead, so we go for a quick third walk of the day.

Once back inside he seems fine, but as Rachel does the final check before we leave, she notices he is shaking once more. I call the vets who say, as there is no vomiting or diarrhoea, we should keep an eye. An impossible task saying no one is there overnight. There is only one thing we can do to make sure the big guy is ok. Rachel looks at me, knowing what we should do, but also understanding the extra pressure it creates. I look back at her, staring into her eyes, knowing I have the support of an amazing woman who understands the sacrifices. I am very lucky to have found my soulmate.

So, juggling the dogs which are already in the van we squeeze Cooper, a large Anatolian Shepherd with a history of biting, into a crate. He is both frightened and curious, a dangerous mix, but I'm glad to say the curiosity wins through in the end.

We pull up back at home and start to unload the van at about half six, just as Haden my three legged epileptic Lurcher goes into a fit. His timing is impeccable and caps off a day which has suddenly become a very difficult one. He compliments that fit with another one at half past ten, with Rachel carrying out clean up duties. We have now been playing the role of carers since six am, a total of over sixteen hours on a day which we lost an hour's sleep the night before because of the change in the clocks.

For the first time I can feel cracks really begin to appear in my exterior. Inside I have been broken for a long time, but now the damage is beginning to display for everyone to see. It feels as if it all is against us right now. A difficult job is becoming more testing by the hour, even the easiest tasks seem to be becoming a challenge. I have been telling everyone that for us to survive we need to take each day at a time. Today though, my mind has changed. If any of us is going to survive this, we must get through the challenges which are laid out before us hour by hour. Every minute we breath feels like a test. From the sublime to the ridiculous, we are under such scrutiny.

Proof of such displayed by this one example. The kennels are situated in an old barn at the back of a working sheep farm. The lockdown has coincided with the beginning of the lambing season. Today as we were trying to get the kennels cleaned, a wayward Ewe ready to give birth at any moment, escapes from the rest of the herd and the pack of obsessive Collies and makes her escape through our big double doors and heads unknowingly into an even bigger pack of dogs. Terrified, she does a lap of the kennels, before exiting through the back door. Every dog of ours is now up a height, the atmosphere has gone from relaxed to manic, chilled to chaos. As I watch Collette chase the pregnant sheep around the barn, not knowing who is the more distressed, I don't know whether to laugh or cry. I stand there frozen by what I have just witnessed, confusion crossed with comedy, I think "you couldn't write this."

Cooper enjoys a walk with Nima, Willow and Indi once we finally make it home. In fact, he is so animated it is both brilliant to see but also difficult to keep him under control. He seems to enjoy sitting outside in the run of his heated kennel, as the night develops into a chill which makes a mockery of the fact the calendar says we have now entered British Summertime.

Something different for him but also a fresh start. I share his uncertainty at what is happening, I feel his anxiety at where he is. However, I cannot lie down and relax like he is. I cannot live in the moment and enjoy the view. I am afraid where this is all going to head.

Day Seven.

Monday 30th March 2020

Total UK Deaths: 1,415

Confirmed Cases: 22,141

I am so tired today. Haden had another fit at 4am this morning, quite a violent one which threw his body off the bed and crashing into the bedside table. A glass was smashed into pieces, splashing water up the walls as far as ceiling. The lamp ended up behind the bed, whilst a picture frame had the piece which supports it so it can stand, bent so much it snapped.

With the fit sometimes comes the urination, which he is completely unaware of. So, the carpet then also needed cleaned. An hour and a half after the fit, we needed to be up. Its day three of our three in. My body is already aching, showing the signs of old age I'm trying my best to ignore, my brain hurts at the thought of trying to comprehend how the day can run as smoothly as possible. I know Collette and Rachel will feel the same, total physical exhaustion coupled with mental fatigue. Though they might deny feeling as old as me! Everyone is worrying about how we are going to survive this, but as I am in charge, I feel the extra responsibility like a noose around my neck. A noose which seems to tighten every single day.

"What is needed at times like this is a strong leader." The words of a volunteer called Jon who helps so much behind the scenes. He has been a huge help to me in the last few months and has a great deal of experience in being involved with charities.

Those words were spoken the Saturday before lockdown as we sat drinking coffee at his house whilst we came up with a plan. The words still ring in my head, but they seem to have been said so long ago now they're more a distant memory than the rallying call I am trying to make them be. The aroma of fresh coffee along with the buzz of dealing with something which was going to be inevitable, I think neither of us expected the world to change so dramatically just 48 hours later.

Cooper seemed ok this morning, in fact I think he really enjoyed the change of scenery and routine. He looked so at home stretching out in the outside run when I opened the curtains, so much so it was a tug on the heart strings to take him back.

 I am still very concerned about him and will be keeping a close eye on him, but on returning to the kennels it felt like we had a stronger bond. He looked for me coming, he initiated the stoke under his chin, he knows we had a special time last night in difficult circumstances and I think he really appreciated it. I know I did. Cooper is one resident which will probably always be with us but being able to handle him like I did last night and give him something different in his life, was a special memory which I will keep with me.

Work is weird right now. There is so much to do with just the three of us in, but of course I have all the other things which my role entails. Sometimes I feel as if the responsibility which comes with what I have created is underestimated by people who think I am just 'messing about on my phone,' but so much else needs to be done.

 My head begins to hurt by early afternoon, and I mean physically not metaphorically. The stress is growing as I try to combine everything and steer the ship in the right direction, whilst not sacrificing any part of me which belongs to the dogs. Jon's 'strong leader' ringing in my ears as a huge Bull Lurcher we have called Jeff drags me around the field like a racehorse pulling the scrap man's cart.

 The pressure intensifies when I receive a phone call to say a dog a volunteer has recently fostered has severely reacted with their other dog, with whom he was cuddled up on the bed with just hours before. The dog is back with us by the afternoon. I just want to shake him and ask him if he realises the fantastic home he has just given up. Lovely people, who thought the world of him. It's so sad he doesn't know what he has just forced himself to lose, or the sadness felt by the two people who love him and wanted to give him so much.

Sheba is not great this afternoon either, her back end seems to have deteriorated even more since this morning. I borrow a support of Oscar to try and give her as much encouragement as I possibly can to walk, but she seems to find it difficult to understand. I'm not sure if it is just strange for her, or whether her dementia makes it a bit more difficult to understand. I will do all I can for her though, I love her so much. Tomorrow we are home, the shifts at the kennels finished for three days. I can spend a little more time with her and try and get her used to it. I can give her everything and all my attention, I can pray she somehow improves and most importantly I can make sure she knows how devoted I am to her battle to survive.

I spend the night on Amazon Prime once more, only this time looking for wheelchairs for dogs. They have reduced so much in price over the years, as I guess more people are open to the idea of using them with their dogs. As all our donated ones are either too small or too big, it means helping her is now affordable and instant.

I know she is ill, I know time is running out, but one thing we do at SHAK is give the dog every opportunity we can. We don't give up on them, we don't throw in the towel and discard them because they aren't able to do what we want any more. We do all we can, no matter what it costs. They've had enough rejection in their lives already.

I hold that thought as I drift off to sleep, exhausted both physically and mentally. I need to rest.

Day Eight.

Tuesday 31st March 2020

Total UK Deaths: 1,808. A rise of 393 in 24 Hours.

Confirmed Cases: 25,150

- 13 year old Ismali Mohamed Abdulwahab is the UK's youngest victim of the Coronavirus. He had no under lying health issues.
- A 12 year old girl dies from COVID-19 in Belgium. Europe's youngest victim of the disease.
- Spain announces 849 deaths in a single day. Its biggest daily rise.

Compared to a normal workday, I treat myself to a bit of a lie in, at least that's what I try and tell myself so I can claim to be relaxing. The truth is I have the alarm set for 8.15am.

The kennels open at 8am and I am anxious about Cooper. I check my phone, no messages or missed calls, which is good. I can never relax or forget about the kennels when I am not there. It has been such an invasive part of my life, which I struggle to let go of for so long now. This global pandemic we are all facing has just amplified the worry and concern. Running this charity has been like raising a child, even as they grow bigger and older and start to look after themselves, the parental instinct is always there.

My intention was to go back to sleep, but then the stretched out, sleeping frame of Sheba on the floor at my side of the bed catches my attention. She is peacefully sleeping and looks so beautiful lain out there in her full glory. You would never be able to tell her back legs no longer work by looking at her now. She looks just like any other German Shepherd, content at being so close to her owner.

I immediately pick my phone back up and open the Amazon app. I have several wheelchairs stored in my virtual basket from last night, so I peruse them again before picking the cheapest one I think is her size.

Swipe to proceed, swipe to proceed, swipe to proceed.

I swipe. It should be here tomorrow. Hopefully, everything will be ok at the kennels and we will still be homebound for the day. That will give us time to get her used to it and see if it helps.

See, there's the instinct again, "hopefully, everything will be ok at the kennels." I am always worried about the kennels when I am not there. Not because of a lack of confidence in my staff, just because the place really has become my life. So much of me has gone into that place, which I will never get back, which means it always seems to be on my mind. I am aware the anxiety for work has begun to intensify over the last twenty four hours.

Those last three days in there were so hard, we all gave everything, but my brain doesn't seem to know when to switch off. I am concerned the worry will get out of hand and become all consuming. I need to be able to focus back onto the admin and funding side of things whilst I am at home. It's the only way I will be turning the negative of worry into the positive of survival. I also need to look after my own mental health.

The rest of the day is spent doing office work. Another Gift Aid claim thanks to the generosity of people responding to the appeal, should bring in just under £600, an incredible amount and such a bonus when we remember that the shop is currently closed.

Which in itself is something I miss a lot in this chaos, the daily fundraising. The security of knowing one day we had raised such and such, but the next we began all over again. The constant stream of funds made us all sleep in our beds at night so much easier. Tomorrow always presented another opportunity. No more waiting a couple of weeks until the next fundraising event, every morning gave us the opportunity to make a big difference. I also started to look at the large amount of emails which have been building up in my inbox. So many, from a wide spectrum of people. Just sorting through them is a task in itself.

      Some are offering support, even if it is just to say they want us to get through this. Some are people offering to foster dogs, which unfortunately just isn't feasible with what is going on right now. Our dogs take a lot of getting to know over many visits. It just isn't safe to operate such a protocol at this present time. Although I appreciate people are suggesting it with the greatest will in the world.

      There are even emails asking us to take peoples dogs and, if we don't, they will have the dog destroyed. I find those ones very hard to take. Surely people understand the rescues are finding it just as tough, if not tougher than your average member of the public? How can we be expected to take on somebody else's problems when we are worried, we won't even last long enough to look after our own?

      It sets my mind raising, fills my heart with worry which I really do not have time or space for right now. I must look after my own mental health I tell myself once more, but it is not so easy. As people's money and savings run out should we brace ourselves for an influx of strays or dogs being taken to the vets to be destroyed, then I'll have the vets on phone looking for me to provide the last opportunity for salvation before death. If this goes on for months or even years, when the money and food become tight, will people just abandon the ones who can't fend for themselves or bring in a wage?

      I know it's my brain going into overdrive again, there are a lot of fantastic, loving pet owners out there, but it is something which I think needs to be at least acknowledged. However, my gut tells me it will be right at the bottom of the list of things for the government to plan for. Some would say rightly so, but then they don't have a gun put to their head, or a life to save via a phone call.

It is also in my head that in the present circumstances, we will not be able to help. The thought of which kills me, but three people to look after fifty dogs every day is already stretching us to the limit. It is impossible to think we could be stretched anymore. The panic begins to kick in again and I can feel my head beginning to have that dull ache of stress. The one which is just always there and doesn't go away, no matter how many tablets you take. I try and move on.

One email I did receive though does put a smile on my face, as despite being so long ago, Dominic Hodgson's Tour De Rescue last summer was a positive move for creating awareness.

He had been reading our appeal and it had reminded him he hadn't sent me the final video of his visit to us.

Watching it back fills me with pride of what I have achieved since my dog Shak died in 2006, but also makes me sad when I look at how uncertain everything is for everybody right now.

Even though it is not yet a year ago, the day the film was made seems like it was shot in a different lifetime. The worries we faced then are nothing compared to what we are fighting against now. Still I put my own personal feelings to one side and upload it to a post which tries to show encouragement and be positive. I want people to remember what we are all about and why people should donate their hard earned money to help us continue to do our work. I really hope it works.

Sky and I have just taken Sheba for a little walk, Sky being my retired Greyhound. I'm hoping it will be easier once the wheels come tomorrow but using the support on her back end will have to do for now.

I know deep down she is dying, but I have to give it one more shot. I have seen at the kennels how much a set of wheels transformed Doyle and then Oscar's lives. Doyle had months longer with us, Oscar is still going. I need to give Sheba the same chance. This has all come on so quickly which is why I am concerned there is something more sinister at hand. Something I will not be able to compete with or make better for her no matter how hard I try.

I look deep into her eyes and see she is tired, but she is always looking for me. I don't know if it is a good sign or a bad sign. For now, I want her to still do and see everything she is used to. Even if it is in shorter quantities.

I'm beginning to cherish every minute she is with me, trying to capture the memories in my brain like a camera does a photograph. File them away for ever, but the fog of knowing what the outcome will be inevitable taints the view.

Teatime arrives and whilst the others are happily tucking into their meals, I take the time to sit with Sheba. She wants to eat but I think the fact she has lost the ability to stand for very long is preying on her mind. So, if the mountain won't come to Mohamed, Mohamed will go to the mountain as they say. I lie down on the floor next to her, hand feeding her favourite wet food with a whole load of pasta, another favourite of hers. We get about two thirds through the meal, then she lets me know she has had enough. I kiss the top of her head and smile. I am very proud of her and the fact she has had a reasonable amount is a positive sign. In reflection, the fact she has eaten anything at all is an amazing achievement.

Standing, I go to get on with the rest of the dogs, she lifts a paw in my direction. I don't know whether it is to say thank you or to say come back, but I smile and drop back to my knees so I can give her a quick cuddle for a little longer. A moment which I capture with that imaginary camera.

She has been so good around all my other dogs, right from the day she arrived, but tonight she is going out on her own. To the others it would seem like we don't go very far, but to Sheba we have just climbed Everest. We stop for a rest and we shoot a little bit of video so I can never forget it, then she goes to the toilet before we make our way home and I lay her out in front of the fire.

You would think most dogs would adore that, it should be their most natural and instinctive place to go and settle, but Sheba has never been one for socialising downstairs with the rest of us, she adores lying under the bed on my side much more. I think she knows eventually I will take my place there and she will know we are all safely settled for the night. I believe with seven other dogs in the house, she is making sure she gets what she considers to be the best spot to sleep.

However, with all that said, I think she really likes her new surroundings tonight. Watching her breath deeply and silently, she drifts away into sleep and somewhere else. I will never know what she is dreaming of, perhaps she is running around a meadow or perhaps she is picturing going just a little further on our walk, but what I do know is, in those dreams she is happy.

Day Nine.

Wednesday 1st April 2020

Total UK Deaths: 563 in one day, taking the total to 2,352.

Confirmed Cases: 29,474

- Spain reports 864 in 24 hours, bringing the total of deaths to 9,053
- France reports 509 fatalities, taking their total to 4,032
- Leading NHS doctor Alfa Saadu dies from COVID-19
- Ministry of Defence calls up 3,000 reservists to fight Coronavirus
- UEFA cancel all Champions League, Europa League and international games until 'further notice.'
- A woman fined £660 for being at Newcastle's Central Station and refusing to tell the Police why she was out.

Today has been the day which all of this has all maybe hit home the most, the feeling of existing on a planet which is dying just seems to have gathered pace. I haven't spoken to anybody who is positive about what we are going through, nobody can see a way out and nobody feels safe.

It really is very scary times, which leaves everybody vulnerable. The fear grows like an uncontrollable mist which crawls across the landscape engulfing everything in its way. Whole families are being torn apart and unable to see each other. Nobody knows how long for, suddenly people are fearing for the lives of loved ones. I can only imagine the fear which ran through families during the World Wars.

The day was supposed to be a positive one for Sheba and me, as her wheelchair was due to arrive by half past eleven.

She woke me up at 4am wanting to go out for a wee, which means her brain is still functioning. Any other time if your dog wakes you up in the middle of the night, you curse. Not now though, the fact she is still responsible for her actions means so much. She is still alive and making decisions. It justifies me doing all I can for her.

On her walk this morning she went to the toilet from both ends, filling my heart with hope we can somehow get her through this. We both sit and await the postman like a child on his or her birthday. I keep getting up to look out the window to see if the red van is approaching any time soon. Settling back down to sit with her, I anxiously look towards the window, before getting up again. Anytime now.

When the post lady does arrive, she brings a load of parcels which my panic buying for the kennels is responsible for. Laundry liquid, dishwasher tablets, dog food, they all arrive alongside Sheba's wheels,

As soon as I unwrap the box my heart sinks, this looks nothing like the item I viewed on the internet. It looks a lot smaller and more fragile; the build quality leaves a lot to be desired. Still I assemble the wheels hoping my gut feeling is wrong. An action of true denial, one of damned determination, my heart tries to tell my head it is wrong. It is not.

Sitting in it, Sheba looks massive. Her back feet trail behind her on the ground, the wheels somewhere near her knees. Although she doesn't know what is going on, she just accepts the change and trundles along, I feel like I have let her down. Failed. Both myself and Rachel measured her and double checked the sizes, we both agreed it would fit. How can you get the measurements of two things so wrong? You can't, I think it is just a poor quality product.

I lay Sheba back in her bed, giving her a peck on the top of her head and telling her "well done." Then I go outside to gather thoughts. I am both disillusioned and angry inside. The sinking feeling of disappointment and uselessness creeps through my body, replacing the hope and motivation which had been bubbling away all morning. I am trying to give her the best chance possible, I am doing everything I can. I know I am, but right now it feels as if it is not enough. I will not let her go without exploring every avenue of making her life better, I cannot afford to get things so wrong. This has really knocked my spirit and made my stomach churn.

Stupid really because it is just a parcel. I will be able to return it and order something else, but delivery is another 48 hours. I'm worried I don't have that long. There is no way I will let her suffer, it just wouldn't be fair or ethical, so I need a quick reaction to this problem. The frustration is almost unbearable.

In normal times I would just hunt down a shop which sells them and travel to get them. I would go anywhere and spend however much I needed to, but in these times, I cannot do that. I am beginning to feel a lot of desperation at the position we are all being made to live in. Even now at home the pressure is beginning to show.

I need to focus, take out my frustration on something else, channel the negative energy into something positive. I look at a pile of old timber which has sat on my drive since the demolition of the old cabin at the kennels this time last year. I go into the garage and produce my saw.

Teatime and Sheba has another bowel of tinned Butchers loaf and pasta. She seems to like it better than any other dog food. I am holding off switching to things like chicken for as long as I can, there is no coming back when you venture down the 'human food' route. I have to hand feed her, but I think the reason for it being that way is she just enjoys the extra attention. As long as she is eating, I don't care. Plus, I like it being that way and so close to her too.

Rachel messages later on to see how she is doing. She shares my disappointment with the chair but is a lot more positive than me. I value what she says so much, the beacon of the lighthouse in the darkness. She tells me to order the other model I was looking at, its three times the price but Sheba is worth it. So, I do.

I ask her about her day, living in the town her days differ so much from mine when we are on our 'non kennels' days. She had gone out to pay some of our donation cheques into the bank and described Morpeth as a ghost town.

"You can't sign anything. The staff all do it for you, and they are only letting two people into the bank at a time. All of the shops are closed apart from food shops and chemists, and they all have queues outside of them. Every other shop window has signs up saying 'Closed' and there is writing all over the pavement thanking people who are doing their best."

I sit and take it all in, it seems like an eternity since I ventured anywhere other than the kennels or the little sleepy village nearest to where I live. I try and picture what it looks like all shut down. The empty car parks, the shutters and the graffiti, then she says something else that makes me listen again.

"So many of the houses have pictures of Rainbows in the windows"

"Rainbows?" I ask, not sure what the relevance is there. "Yes rainbows." She replies "People, especially the ones with children, have been making rainbows and putting them in the windows for people to see."

"Why rainbows?" Still unaware of the significance, although I do like the idea of all the colours in such a dark time. Then the penny drops.

"To show a sign of hope." She says. Hope, now there is a word which I haven't heard or thought of for a long time.

Day Ten.

Thursday 2nd April 2020

Total UK Deaths: 569 more deaths taking total to 2,921

Confirmed Cases: 33,718

- Coronavirus patients may have ventilators taken away and given to patients more likely to survive according to new guidelines issued to UK Doctors.
- 23 year old man jailed for a year for spitting at two police officers and claiming he had COVID-19.
- A six week old baby in Connecticut dies from Coronavirus. The world's youngest victim.
- More than a million cases of Corona Virus confirmed worldwide.
- Comedian Eddie Large (part of Little and Large) dies after contracting COVID-19 in hospital.
- The government unveils a five point action plan to achieve 100,000 COVID-19 tests per day in England by the end of April.

The wind howls through my bedroom window, reminding me of the months of darkness which have supposedly passed. Could the cold, dark chill of winter have returned? I always sleep with the windows open, with nothing but fields for miles, I never draw the curtains. I like to see the purples and gold of the sunrise.

Today I don't see those though, instead I see the sheen of my opaque voiles fluttering in another world. The dangerous outside world, where the wind howls drown out the sound of the lambs. I wonder if I lean out of the window, whether it would blow me away to another time.

Within an instant of waking I am reminded I am living through what could be the end of the world, the weather just sets the tone. Like the morning after the night before when you have consumed too much alcohol, the harshness of what is going on hits home one by one. As I sit on the edge of my bed, I try and prepare myself for another day, both mentally and physically.

Sheba goes out for her toilet, I have to hold her at all times, then she quite happily tucks into hand fed Butchers Tripe loaf with a little pasta. It is heart-breaking to be part of, but she seems to enjoy her breakfast, so I tell myself it is ok, burying the pain and anguish deep inside for now. As long as she is eating and enjoying it, I keep telling myself, but I know what is coming. I have been in this heart breaking position so many times before. I am so proud of her, but my stomach gurgles with the sickly feeling of knowing.

Today is my last day of being home based, it's incredible how time flies right now. Reminiscent of school holidays many years ago when you think on day one you have forever off. Then, as the days pass, you realise you still haven't done your homework. Before you know it, it is the Sunday night ritual of bath, hair wash and early night for school. An early night coupled with an early rise. My life is currently being split between school and school holidays.

Trying to plan for the week ahead I venture into Rothbury to try and pick up some shopping, plus to post an order for one of my other books. I really don't know how to describe the sight which meets me. This normally vibrant tourist hub is so quiet.

Only the local co-op, butchers and the Post Office remain open. There are no hordes of people sitting on the benches looking at the flower displays, no gangs of bikers taken root outside the fish and chip shop. The 'closed' signs which Rachel described last night, are everywhere. The whole place is indeed like a ghost town.

I collect my shopping, sticking to the guidelines in yellow and black tape on the floor. Two metres apart, that's the rule, but how do you do that in a tiny supermarket which is heaving with desperate people grabbing whatever food they can. Yes, Rothbury might be a ghost town, but being the nearest thing to supermarket for miles around, the ghouls have congregated there, taking all they can.

As I stand in the queue so I can pay, I take the opportunity to 'people watch' my fellow shoppers. Some are almost measuring out two metres without the yellow markings, others seem oblivious to what they mean and dance around the threshold like it was a bed of hot coals. They know they mean something, but their brain just can't comprehend what. The desire for the tuna sandwich and diet coke in their hands is just too much. They are even prepared to risk their lives for them, unfortunately it also puts others at risk, but they don't realise the potential consequences of their actions. The pains of hunger seem more important.

Then you have the masks and latex gloves brigade. They look like something from an apocalyptic movie, knowing they are safe from whichever surface they choose to put their hands on. Unaware however, those gloves could be riddled with the virus from everything they touch, therefore spreading it like a rash for everybody else. At least inside the latex though, they are safe. Self-preservation forget everybody else.

I sanitise my hands just watching them. I want the cashier to hurry up, to serve the three people in front of me so I can leave this pit of germs. Maybe I should have worn a mask and gloves too, maybe I just shouldn't have come.

I return home, squirting the liquid sanitiser everywhere, my hands, my shopping bags, my shopping, then the phone starts.

One of the volunteers has just had a week's holiday with her father. He is a paramedic, so on the front line and a hero. He was sent home from work yesterday with a high temperature, so a COVID-19 test was taken. His results have just come back positive. The first person I actually know to have been confirmed.

Obviously, the main thing is he and his family are safe and he makes a good recovery, but it also confirms to me I made the right decision in putting the kennels into lockdown. The volunteer was supposed to be in last weekend. If she shows symptoms it would have put the whole operation in trouble.

The next message doesn't make any better reading, in fact it is really sad. Mona has been unwell for a little while, but today Michael who also volunteers, told me they had had to say goodbye.

Mona arrived from Birmingham on the very day that I got the keys to our kennels. Such was the urgency to get her to us, so she avoided being put to sleep, I thought 'well we're here now, why not.' She hated everything and everybody, which is why I instantly fell in love with her and her 'teenage' attitude. She was a rebel in her own right, I guess she reminded me of myself.

Her arrival was about twelve years ago, and the miserable and aggressive little Staffy eventually mellowed and spent her last days with Michael, Alison and their other SHAK dog Bubbles.

The vet suspected a brain tumour was responsible for her fitting and sudden change of behaviour, nothing could be done, other than to give her a whole load of love, which I know she got tenfold.

I feel for everyone who is involved in the pain and worry felt by both families. Such special people, each and every one of them, who have given so much to SHAK over the years. Whilst I am here hurting and making the tough decisions, they have been shut out for safety, but still they are facing the darkness of the days we are living in right on the frontline. My heart goes out to them all.

I look at Sheba lying in front of the fire, as the daylight disappears unlike the wind. Casting my gaze further afield I see Sky, Keiser, Henry and Bandit, all enjoying the warmth and the company of being with each other. No masks, no gloves, no two metres, simply relaxing and enjoying life. Oblivious to the dangers of the world outside, no recognition of how vulnerable I am right now, or how delicate the charity's position is. I watch them all snoring and legs twitching, deep in sleep. I don't know whether to smile or cry, but I do feel very proud.

Day Eleven.

Friday 3rd April 2020

Total UK Deaths: 684 die in 24 hours taking the total to 3,605

Confirmed Cases: 38,168

- NHS nurses Areema Nasreen (36) Aimee O'Rourke (39) die after testing positive for COVID-19.
- Mother of the UK's youngest Coronavirus victim, Ismail Mohamed Abdulwahab (13) misses her sons funeral after two siblings develop symptoms of COVID-19.
- Government urge the public to stay at home as temperatures predicted to hit 18c on Sunday.

Another day of mixed emotions, as I resume my three day rota at the kennels. It's always so good to see the dogs again, but also very stressful to try and blend all my roles along with the most basic one of getting the dogs out and cleaned. I sometimes think it is forgotten just how much pressure comes with running an organisation like this, maybe I was asking too much of myself and the others on my team for me to do both roles. I can see at times they think "what is he doing now?" but without the organisation and managing there wouldn't be a charity for them to work for. Likewise, I gave up my business to work with dogs, not to be sat in an office. Sometimes it just feels as if it is all too much.

The morning gets off to a bit of an emotional start, as for the first time Sheba doesn't fancy her pasta, butcher's loaf or even the chicken soup she enjoyed yesterday. The lack of appetite is one thing, I can handle that, I am more concerned that she doesn't want a drink. My head starts to race away with various scenarios and what could happen. Refusing food and water always seems to be the sign that indicates the beginning of the end. It is just gone six am and already I can feel my stress levels rise.

Once at the kennels, she takes up her position next to my desk, that way she can see me every time I enter the office area. I give her a cuddle, about to go and get Keene out for a walk, then without thinking I offer her a Bonio biscuit. She takes it and devours it, so I offer her another one. She takes it too. After the breakfast shenanigans, it is just great to see her eating. So, throughout the day I keep offering her a treat. Amazingly the Bonio's progress to dried liver, to rich tea biscuits. She takes them all, consuming more calories than she has for days. Whilst I accept it isn't a great diet, she is eating. There is just a very slight glimmer of hope in my heart.

A few days ago, I admitted to panic buying things I thought we might need if this crisis goes on for longer than the initial three weeks. Thankfully, a volunteer called Paul does a lot of our food collections from places such as pet shops and warehouses. When we don't have room at the kennels, or if we have an abundance of supplies, he tends to stock any excess in the two garages which he has access too.

Paul does a lot of running around for us and is very much a 'go to man' if we need anything. When I asked him how much food he had stored, he offered to spend his day off bringing it up. Then by chance, another volunteer Jax moved to a new house this morning with her husband Darron. When they heard about the stock piling, they contacted Paul and offered to use the Luton van they had on hire to bring it all up in one go. In doing so it saved Paul several journeys, but also reduced the risk of any infection. He admitted afterwards he was worried about coming up in case he took any germs back home to his father who is in his nineties. Sensible, but also a reminder to us all about what is happening in the bigger outside world and how much at risk we all are.

So, the afternoon was spent filling the spaces in the food store which Collette had made just this morning. It meant we were a little behind, but also eased any worries of the food supplies running out. Another worry which had been circulating somewhere in the back of my battered brain for several days, had been dealt with. A tiny bit of pressure lifted somewhere.

Today was another example of amazing teamwork and a perfect display of the support we have waiting in the wings once this is all over.

Once everyone was gone, Rachel and I tried Sheba in Oscar's wheelchair just to get a rough idea of how she would take to it. I was worried she might be too weak for her front legs to pull her along. Oscar makes it look so easy, but then again, he is an incredibly inspirational dog.

At first, she was very wary and not sure what was going on, but after a couple of metres she got into it and powered herself all the way to the van, trying to get herself back home. For the second time today, her actions filled my heart with a little more hope. If you looked deep enough into my eyes you may have even seen rainbows like in the house windows in Morpeth. Once we got home, she had a big drink of water, then rolled on her back in her bed, content, exhausted and I think she was a little proud of herself.

Her own set of wheels had arrived, thanks to the key workers at Amazon Prime, so whilst I prepared the feeds and sorted our other dogs, Rachel built up Sheba's chariot. It was dark when it was finished and we finally got her out for a test drive, and although she wasn't quite Queen Boudica racing behind her horses, she put her heart and soul into going those few yards. Another matter of worry checked off the list.

This morning I was full of self-doubt and defeat. Nothing has changed, her health will not improve I know, and it hurts so much, but if we can give her just a little bit more mobility and thus time. I can't think of anything else right now. I have to be as determined as she is.

Such is the desire to help her, the funds for wheelchair have been donated, again more support which means so much to our beliefs.

Finally, we all retire to bed exhausted from the day we have just shared. I am writing this, desperately trying to keep my eyes open. Sheba is flat out on the floor next to me; she looks so worn out but peaceful. Her back legs are kicking like dogs do when they dream, I go to sleep hoping she is practising being in her chair.

Day Twelve.

Saturday 4th April 2020

Total UK Deaths: 708 deaths in 24 hours, taking total to 4,313

Confirmed Cases: 41,903

- 5 year old child included in the new figures, Britain's newest youngest victim.
- Spain report 809 new deaths, the second day in a row the amount of deaths has dropped. In total 11,744.
- Boris Johnson's pregnant fiancée Carrie Symonds spent the last week in bed with symptoms of Coronavirus.

One of the biggest realisations in running the kennels the way we have to right now, is acknowledging we are literally stretched to the limit. The luxury of having six or seven people in or somebody arriving to help speed things up in the afternoon is now gone.

Imagine then the feeling of helplessness and panic, when I arrive at 8am to find Collette looking a worrying shade of grey, having been up during the night vomiting.

It's a huge credit to her that she made the journey in to work. Not wanting to let me and Rachel down, or more importantly the dogs, had motivated her to turn in. Great commitment which is exactly what we need and very much appreciated. It shows how much the team want us to get through this without the dogs losing out on too much.

There is also the other side I keep mentioning, manging the organisation and evaluating each situation. I took one look at how ill she looked and knew I had to send her back home.

Obviously, her health and wellbeing are of great importance, and we need her back fighting fit as soon as possible, but if it's a bug of some sort and it was to be passed on to Rach or myself, the whole project will collapse.

Next issue of course is the job is just too big for two people. With fifty dogs all needing fed twice, cleaned out and walked twice, there is no way even the minimum of the daily routine could get done with just two staff members. Once again, I have a difficult decision looming over me.

I feel the sickly sense of dense, thick fog travel behind my eyes from temple to temple. Pressure, pressure, pressure. The word itself seems to bray of each side of my skull like a man striking a gong. Every time he hits it, the noise merges into the ripple of the hit before. My head feels like it is going to explode, and I have to sit down and take a moment.

We can either struggle and cheat the dogs out of their second walks, hoping we are even able to complete the first ones and all the cleaning. Or I can take a bit of a risk and ask one of the volunteers to step in, meaning the sanitisation and cleanliness takes on an even more important role in our day. Paranoia takes over from pressure. It seems almost ridiculous to think the introduction of just one more person into our little world of six could make such a difference and become such a worry, but it does. It's another door open to the outside world and the invisible danger which is lurking there.

When the outcome of a lockdown became apparent, I approached Jax to see if she would be our 'go to' in times just like this. Retired and living only ten minutes away, she confirmed she would be able to step in at the drop off a hat. The hat just dropped.

Within the hour Collette had retired to bed at home, Jax had turned in and Rachel had worked so hard to make sure the cleaning wasn't too far behind. Great teamwork and incredible commitment to these dogs once again

I have said it before, but they really don't know what is going on. Whilst we are doing all we can to keep their routine, their days have changed, and their worlds become a little bit smaller. If nothing else, they will have noticed us running around more stressed. Yet they have reacted incredibly, remain as well behaved as 50 rescue dogs with behavioural issues can!

Sheba had her first venture out in her new wheels this afternoon, I think it was a very strange experience for her, but hopefully it is something she will get used to and will help her to stay with me. I really feel so helpless, yet I know I am doing all I can, it just feels like it isn't enough.

She ate the best she has for days today, and her toileting is normal, so that is all positive, but she gets so tired.

Mind, she is not the only one. Five thirty start and an eight thirty finish by the time all the jobs with the dogs here are sorted, rubbish burnt (another issue as all the tips are closed) we collapse into bed. Somehow, we got there today and survived to tell the tale, that's all that matters. We have it all to do again tomorrow.

Day Thirteen.

Sunday 5th April 2020

Total UK Deaths: 621 deaths in 24 hours, total now 4,934

Confirmed Cases: 47,806

- Boris Johnson admitted to hospital for tests as he still has persistent symptoms and a high temperature.
- Queen likens this crisis to the wartime spirit she experienced in historic address to the nation.
- Health Secretary Matt Hancock warns Britons outdoor exercise maybe banned unless people confirm to social distancing rules.
- Italy records its lowest daily death toll in two weeks, with a total of 525 in 24 hours. Taking the country's total to 15, 887. The number of confirmed cases also is a lower rise than the day before, from 124,632 to 128,984.

The days are all beginning to blur into one now. Today is Sunday, but it feels no different to any other day we have been in work. Before all of this happened, it was the day I saw my daughter, the day we spent time together as a family, the day there was always football on the TV. Instead driving into work feels like I am the only person on this earth. Other key workers may have Sundays off, I don't know, but the roads this morning are even more ghostly.

    Collette is still off; it seemed the sensible thing to do giving she would then have another three days to rest. Once again Jax steps up and comes in for the full day.

    In her previous role as a volunteer it has always just been about walking the dogs and getting them out for days. Two days running now she has been scrubbing kennels and dealing with the messy side. Hard work and less glamourous, there are the same levels of self-satisfaction knowing you have given the dog nice clean bedding to rest in. I think she has enjoyed herself, despite the fact she too has climbed into nice comfortable bedding nearly as soon as she got home. When all this is over, she will be able to look back on these two days as valuable experience and insight into what others do. I think such knowledge is essential in building a successful team.

Sheba is still trying to get used to the wheels, but once we get down the bumpy farm track and into the smooth tarmacked exercise area, she is a lot more comfortable and is able to complete a full lap before steering her way back to the van. She is getting good at letting me know when she has had enough.

In the outside world things are really beginning to become a worry. People are ignoring the pleas for social distancing, gathering in parks, sunbathing, having group picnics, in the first warm weather of the year.

The ignorance of others is costing people their lives. I find it so hard to comprehend, it's as if the reality of what is happening hasn't quite sunk in with some. Ignore it and it will go away seems to be the approach.

Setting off for home from the kennels, we head into Alnwick so I can pick up mail from the office. On the way, just before the castle, there is a layby which is usually occupied by young drivers and their cars. You know the type, not doing any harm just congregating.

Despite what is going on and the constant warnings, the boys are still there as we pass. Leaning out of their windows or standing in circles together. No social distancing, no two metres apart. I shake my head as we pass. I wonder how many of those will become infected or know people who will. I doubt if it will even sink in that it could all be their fault.

At the office there are twenty one envelopes addressed to either me or SHAK. All of the envelopes seem white, for once there doesn't look to be any bills. I am too tired after another fifteen hour shift to start sifting through them today, hopefully they will make a good start to an admin day tomorrow.

Day Fourteen.

Monday 6th April 2020

Total UK Deaths: 439 new deaths, taking the total to 5,373

Confirmed Cases: 51,608

- Boris Johnson's condition deteriorates as he is rushed into intensive care
- Japan declares states of emergency over Coronavirus
- More than 4,100 have died in New York alone as refrigerated lorries are being used as makeshift morgues to deal with the body count. US surgeon general Jerome Adams describes the sight as "our Pearl Harbour moment, our 9/11 moment."
- Later it is announced that bodies maybe buried temporarily in parks because the city's morgues are full. Plans to dig trenches so that 10 caskets can be buried in a line are discussed.
- In Spain, deaths have slowed for the fourth day in a row.

The support we have had from the public during this crisis has been incredible, but as I start to open those envelopes this morning, I really do begin to understand how greatly appreciated our work is.

Heartfelt letters and cards accompany a pile of cheques, every single penny of which will make a difference in our battle for survival.

There are a lot of comments about the article which was published by the Northumberland Gazette or the piece I did on Radio Newcastle, but the main theme that reoccurs time and time again is "where would the dogs be without SHAK."

Something I don't need to answer but serves as a gentle reminder of what this is all about and why we are fighting so hard for it all to stay alive.

I do a tally up after all the post has been opened. In those envelopes alone there is £7,140 in donations, taking the total since the appeal started to £18,079.

Figures which are beyond my wildest dreams. Support I find so humbling when all I have ever tried to do is the right thing and I can't emphasise how grateful I am. It gives us breathing space to know that we will be able to survive a little longer. A bit of hope we will make it and come through the other side. The thought of which brings another worry. We are safe now, but we have no idea how long this is going to go on for, or how much money we will need.

Day Fifteen.

Tuesday 7th April 2020

UK Deaths: Rise of 786 deaths, taking the total to 6,159
Confirmed Cases: 55,242

- Boris Johnson still in intensive care and receiving oxygen support.
- China reports no COVID-19 deaths for the first time during the outbreak. Authorities began releasing reported daily deaths all the way back in January.
- Other European countries such as Norway, Denmark, Czech Republic and Austria have all started to relax coronavirus lockdown restrictions, with schools in Denmark due to reopen on 15th April.
- Man reported to have attacked three Police Officers and a Police Dog with a plank of wood with nails sticking out of it, after they question whether his journey was essential as he tried to board a train at Nottingham Railway Station.
- A man who deliberately coughed on two Police Officers saying he hoped that they passed COVID-19 onto their children is jailed for 19 weeks.
- Bodies are being wrapped in sheets due to an alleged shortage of body bags in Surrey it is claimed.

It seems as if the whole country is descending into absolute chaos, whilst elsewhere in the world things are beginning to work out. You have to ask is this because of society's absolute defiance to follow lockdown regulations. Or are we simply just a little bit behind the others in terms of the virus running its course and going into lockdown too late. I know my feelings on the subject.

A trip to Rothbury to buy stamps of all things, to post thank you letters for donations is like a trip into the abyss. People everywhere wearing masks and latex gloves. I even pass somebody driving his car with gloves on. I'm no expert, but surely all the germs which have been collected on the latex are now spread all over his steering wheel. The world has gone mad.

It would appear the strain and stress are beginning to show amongst our workforce too. People's pay packets are suddenly becoming smaller as the knock on effect from the three on, three off rota begins to take hold.

There isn't a great deal we can do, as the Government has so far offered no help whatsoever to charities, especially animal organisations, so all we can do is abide by the Governments guidelines on social distancing and hope this crazy time is over soon.

I can both empathise and sympathise with the staff who are obviously worried their mortgages and bills will suffer, my own business The Rescue Place which offers a stray dog collection service for the local council during out of hours, has been off the road since we went into lockdown too. The result of which has affected my income and the same for the people who work for me.

It is a real worry and I am wary of ripples of unrest, fully understand them, but as a charity the situation remains out of our control. The whole world is suffering.

Day Sixteen.

Wednesday 8th April 2020

Total UK Deaths: 938 taking the total to 7,097

Confirmed Cases: 60,733

- Prime minister still in intensive care but is responding to treatment, Downing Street has said. Boris Johnson has now been in hospital for 3 nights.
- The temporary mortuary in Birmingham airport has already started storing bodies, even though its conversion isn't finished yet.
- Wales takes things into their own hands and extends its lockdown to beyond the Easter weekend.
- A man is jailed for three months after stealing surgical masks from a hospital in London.
- Two men who licked their hands before wiping them on meat, fresh food and fridge handles in a supermarket in Morecambe, are being hunted down by Police.
- 14 transport workers have now died in London after contracting COVID-19. Raising questions whether public transport should still be in operation.
- Wuhan the city that became the epicentre of the global crisis of the coronavirus, has ended its lockdown after 11 weeks. A huge party and light show were put on for its 11 million residents.
- A four year old Malayan Tiger in a Bronx zoo has tested positive for COVID-19. Nadia was tested after showing symptoms of the virus after being in contact with a keeper (unnamed) who was also tested positive.

Another day of number crunching and looking at options, as the Government are still no further forward in announcing whether the national lockdown will be lifted after the three weeks first stipulated by Boris Johnson. I really don't see how they can be, considering the death toll is rising on a daily basis still. It would, in my opinion be foolish to relax anything as the virus would surely then just reignite its reign of terror.

The consequences for SHAK though if it is extended, means we will have to continue on as we are in our very own lockdown.

Volunteers would still be not be able to attend, whilst full time staff would have to continue on reduced paid hours, with the part time staff being asked to continue to volunteer extra days. All this of course would allow us to continue with our model of two teams working three days in and three days out.

There are so many things to consider, but ultimately, we have to follow the guidelines set by the Government on social distancing. We must abide by the rules, as a charity we have to act responsibly for our staff and keep them safe, which in turn protects the dogs.

A video What's App group call, which seems to be the way the majority of meetings are done these days, between myself, Joan, and Jon, gives us an opportunity to discuss things almost face to face.

We cover every angle, including how the Governments furlough choice isn't really an option as the level of work is still there, in fact there is an even greater demand with us operating shorthanded. We look at various ways of changing rota's and hours, whilst we all agree that the current segregation of teams has to stay in place for now. That is imperative.

Likewise, we understand people have mortgages and bills to pay along with families to support. In the cases of two members of staff, they are dropping up to two day's wage on some weeks. There is no denying such a loss is a big hit on anybody's pay packet.

So, we try to come up with an alternative. Obviously, we cannot just pay people for not coming to work, this organisation relies on donations to pay wages and we cannot waste the public's hard earned money in such a way. As Trustees we have a responsibility to make sure the charity's funds are used correctly and wisely.

Instead we come up with a scheme where we offer staff who are currently losing pay the chance to take those days as paid leave, which will be deducted from their annual holiday entitlement. Of course, they still would have the option to take unpaid leave and save their holidays or take a mixture of both. It would be entirely up to them and also could be utilised to be to their benefit on every count. Maybe they could top up the weeks they only get paid for three days by taking two days paid leave. Then on the weeks they get paid for four days, perhaps they can muddle through. Or of course they could just take one days paid leave that week.

The Trustees and Jon all agree in a climate where people are losing their jobs on a daily basis, it is a very generous and considerate offer, one we hope the people effected will embrace.

In the afternoon I write a post to update our supporters about what is going on and the fact we are still here. My intentions are to make everybody realise their support has been essential in our survival, but we need it to continue for as long as this gloom and disease hovers over the country.

"I just thought I would give you all a little update to say that we are still here and doing our best to survive in these worrying days. I hope everyone out there is safe and well too.

The response to the appeal I launched (which seems like a lifetime ago) has been nothing short of sensational. The generosity of people from all over the world means we now have the resources to go on for several months, by which hopefully this terrible time will have improved and we can start looking at going back to normal. We have also been successful with an application to Support Adoption for Pets through being partnered to the Alnwick Pets at Home store. An emergency grant should be arriving in the next few days.

Knowing all of that gives us inspiration to continue to do our work the best that we can.

We are already setting things in place for the recovery period, with big news on our retail side, a new book called 'Rescue In Lockdown' and an amazing opportunity to win a Porsche 911 Cabriolet that has been donated to us..... See I told you the support has been amazing!

On a daily basis, the lockdown has hit us quite hard, as we work alongside the government's guidelines for social distancing. All of our volunteers have been very understanding, although it is very frustrating for them to have to stay away. The staff have also made some great sacrifices by either reducing their paid hours or volunteering more depending on what they are contracted to. Including myself, this has then provided us with two teams of 3 that work 3 days on and then 3 days off. Very hard work, but essential to try and reduce the risk of spreading any virus.

It is a great testament to everyone's dedication that, despite having 50 dogs to look after, their routine of being fed twice and outside twice has continued. Whilst there isn't as much contact as normal, the dogs seem extremely happy still. It's as if they know that something in the wider world is going on and we are doing all we can.

We have stocked up on all supplies and have an abundance of food, so again we should be ok for a while, although I think the Amazon drivers are sick of driving to my house!

So, all in all, things are ok for now. The uncertainty of when this will be over or when lockdown conditions will ease, means that nobody can really stop worrying. Pulling together as a team of supporters and as the teams at the kennels means we are doing all we can whilst we wait. The charity and the dogs will always be grateful for that.

If you would like to donate to help us in this time of crisis, you can by sending a cheque made payable to SHAK to SHAK HQ, Greenwell Road, Alnwick NE66 1HB or via Paypal:

https://www.paypal.me/shaksanctuary

Stay safe, stay indoors and thank you."

I close the post with a picture of a rainbow over the field in which we walk the dogs. At the time it was just a pretty view, now every time I look at it, I can hear Rachel's words echoing inside my head. "To show a sign of hope." She said, which is exactly what I was trying to do with the post I wrote.

At home I am trying to just get on with things and make the most of some beautiful weather. Between meetings, phone calls and emails I get the grass and some of the hedge cut.

The last of my panic buying from last week arrives on a huge lorry in the shape of twenty one, twenty five litre bottles of kennel disinfectant. Unwrapping the plastic which has been protecting the containers so tightly, then 'hand balling' all twenty one into the van ready for my first shift 'on' tomorrow is exhaustive and thirsty work.

Once it's done, I open a well-deserved beer and carry Sheba out to join me. She is still fighting and enjoying the extra company and attention she is receiving on our days at home, but I can see she is weak. She is eating still, dog food too, although she has developed an incredible liking for rich tea biscuits.

However, I know she isn't really eating enough. She has been out on several little trips in her wheels, but she finds it so exhausting. I think her mental condition makes it extra hard for her brain to compute she can still use her front legs, or even what her front legs are for, but she is trying, which means the world to me.

She barks when she wants something and still lets me know during the night if she needs to go out. I have moved her up onto my bed with me and Haden, just so I don't sleep through her wanting to be out. She seems to like that, especially considering she chose all her time living here to be under the bed. I like it too, I love having her so close, but also because she gives great cuddles.

    I know it must be so hard for her to accept all the changes, but she isn't telling me she is ready to leave us yet. I've always said just because I am the one that holds the lead, it doesn't make me God. Sheba will let me know when it's time.

Day Seventeen.

Thursday 9th April 2020

Total UK Deaths: 881 taking total to 7,978

Confirmed Cases: 65,077

- Lockdown to stay in place for the foreseeable future and certainly over the Easter weekend. Of which, the Government have made a plea for people to stay at home to prevent the virus from having "a second chance to kill more people."
- Boris Johnson moves out of intensive care.
- Abdul Mabud Chowdhury, the doctor who wrote to the prime minister three weeks ago to warn him that health workers needed more PPE (Personal Protective Equipment) dies from COVID-19.
- Ada Zanusso, an Italian lady of 103 is reported as surviving the coronavirus even though doctors thought she was doomed.
- Police shut down 494 house parties in Greater Manchester which included fireworks and DJ's.

The day started out like all the others at the kennels. The routine we have set in place works, but it also means every day is exactly the same. I honestly have no idea what day it is, or even what month any more to be honest. I'm sure everyone feels the same.

We get the day off to the usual start, frantic but organised, then we hit a setback. The water goes off. Thankfully, I was warned by a text late last night from the landlord, so we had filled as many buckets as we could in preparation. I could see the resignation on the faces of Collette and Rachel when the taps dried up. This job is hard enough as it is at the moment without having any running water to change the dogs drinking bowls or use a hose. Hopefully, we had filled enough buckets to at least get the kennels into some sort of clean state. It felt as if it was the icing on the cake, the world was against us. We had only been at work two hours, but already we needed a lift.

Then my phone beeped to say our PayPal account had received another donation. Wrestling Zeus into the back run at the time, I glanced at my phone. A couple who have given us tremendous support over the last couple of years had seen my post from yesterday. They were thrilled at the fact we have received such a positive response, delighted all the hard work which had gone on at many different levels had secured our future for now. So, with that in mind they had decided to donate £3,000.

My heart stopped for a second, of that I'm sure. If somebody who lives half the country away from us can have so much faith in our ability to get through this, then having a temporary loss of water shouldn't knock our spirits.

After telling the others, we got the kennels cleaned in record time, the water came back on just over an hour later. The moment my phone beeped and the inspiration it gave us, will be one of the moments I will not forget when this is all done.

Whilst the Government seem to be doing absolutely nothing for animal charities and their workers in this moment of crisis, some of the organisations who have supported us over the years understand exactly what we are up against and are doing all they can, in whatever way they can.

A couple of weeks ago, Support Adoption for Pets, which is the charitable trust side of Pets at Home, announced they would be offering emergency grants to animal charities during such a difficult period. As we are partnered with the Alnwick branch, we thought it would be worth a punt.

Volunteer Jon, who has been so valuable offering advice and beavering away behind the scenes looking for any form of update from the powers that be or funding opportunities we may be eligible for, offered to put in an application.

Just a couple of hours after my PayPal notification, Support Adoption for Pets paid £5,000 into our bank account. It was a feeling of utter disbelief which filled my heart. Such amazing generosity and faith in our beliefs had given us even more light at the end of the tunnel. The tally of £8,000 raised in a couple of hours had just secured our future for even longer. It all felt as if it was a dream, as if my brain was somehow trying to trick me into believing we were going to be ok.

Next up was a delivery of two pallets of food from Butchers, the dog food company. We have benefitted from their amazing generosity in the past, but last week they contacted Trustee Joan to see if we wanted an extra delivery of food given the circumstances. As I keep saying, nobody knows how long this is going to last, especially after the uncommitted announcement made by Dominic Raab in the prime minister's absence tonight, of when the lockdown will end. Their very kind offer was gratefully accepted.

So, this afternoon, a freight lorry packed with tinned food arrived, all free of charge. It takes our food supplies to the next level, especially after last week's pulling together of all the resources we already had dotted around. We now have enough food to last months rather than weeks, which is in itself a mind crushing worry lifted.

However, I should have known it was all too good to be true. Just as the second pallet was being unloaded from the lorry, the driver happened to comment about the weight which was on there.

"I certainly wouldn't want to handball it in, that's for sure." I replied, the end of the word 'sure' coming out of my mouth just as the contents of pallet toppled over and off the tail lift, landing all over the farmyard.

Accidents happen, and I was able to see the funny side after I had carried 90 boxes of 24 tins into the barn by myself, then placing it back on the pallet it had ejected itself from. Never have I felt such pride at a stack of dog food.

Just as I was finishing, Sheba barked from my office to let me know she wanted to go out for the toilet. I got her out and she did what she had to do, but just as she was settling down in her bed, I noticed her vulva was swollen and there were little droplets of blood. I was sure it wasn't like that this morning, so took a photograph and sent it to our vet Emily. She was immediately on the phone asking questions. Of course, with this lockdown, it is the way that vets are conducting most of their consults, but Emily always goes that extra mile for us. A few more pictures and videos later, it was concluded it may be one of three things.

Firstly, it could be that Sheba is in season, which considering we haven't seen any signs of this in the two years she has been with us, plus her age, it seems an option which is unlikely.

Secondly, it could be a UTI (Urinary Tract Infection) which could possibly lead to why she went off her back legs so suddenly and why she is so wobbly in general.

Thirdly, it could be a Pyometra (infection of the womb) in which case we have a very serious condition.

The fact Sheba is alert and still eating would go against the Pyo theory. Nina, an old Malinois we had, suffered from one and I saw just how flat it made her. Also, the blood from the vagina would be more of a pussy discharge.

All of the above and given her age, we decided to try a series of elimination of the easier options first.

As the surgery is closed and she lives not far from me, Emily offered to put up some antibiotics to treat a water infection, then leave them on her doorstep for me to pick up on my way home.

It was whilst chatting to her on the phone, once again the severity of what is happening in the world suddenly hit home. She had had to go to the surgery because a very old dog was seriously ill. I didn't ask what was wrong, but the conclusion was the little guy was put to sleep.

Such a hard decision and awful thing to go through at the best of times. Something which is never easy and a memory you will never forget. However, because of the current situation it was made even worse for this poor family. For lockdown safety they weren't allowed in the building. They had to watch their beloved pet and best friend slip away out of their lives forever through the surgery window whilst standing outside.

Day Eighteen.

Friday 10th April 2020

Total UK Deaths: 980 new deaths, meaning total is now 8,958

Confirmed Cases: 70,272

- UK's new death total in 24 hours surpasses the highest amount of daily deaths so far of both Spain (961) and Italy (919) whilst todays victims were between 27 and 100 years old.
- Global death toll has now surpassed 100,000.
- Chief nurse announces new emergency Nightingale hospitals in Exeter and Sunderland.
- Ireland and Italy both extend lockdowns, but no official decision from the UK until next week.
- Celtic legend Kenny Dalglish the latest celebrity to test positive and is now in hospital receiving treatment for COVID-19.
- Boris Johnson can walk again after being relocated from intensive care to a hospital ward.
- In New York City, extra graves are being dug in cemeteries, as pictures show pine caskets stacked on top of each other in huge burial pits.

Good Friday, the start of Easter Weekend. Probably the lowest day I have encountered in this pandemic so far.

I haven't seen my daughter or mother for over three weeks now and I am beginning to feel isolated and alone. As I was scheduled to work all weekend before this happened, I had booked holiday for Saturday to take my daughter out for the day and it obviously isn't going to happen now because it would go against every rule of lockdown. Plus, in an ironic twist of fate, the way the shifts have fallen, I'm at work.

My spirits are beginning to fail me, the metaphorical rainbow is hidden so far behind the thick black storm clouds, it may as well not be there. An all-consuming, typhoon of a whirl wind has taken its place and sucked every piece of positivity and hope away, maybe for good. The rain has come to cloud my vision, washing away the memories and the motivation. Hurricane season is upon us.

I can feel the frustration and anger so many others must be feeling at being confined to their own homes, I feel their anguish at not being able to do as they wish.

We are all living as if we are prisoners, I fully understand the importance of why, but today is the first time the loneliness of how I am living and the tiny world in which I am operating, has begun to affect my mental state. I remember saying some days ago, when all this started, I had to look after my own mental health. Today I feel like clarity is lost and I am heading into a dark hole which has no way out. I wonder how many other people are feeling the same.

The pressure has begun to get too much. Too consuming and devouring, the frustration seems to have gotten to some members of staff too. There is an undercurrent of unhappiness as we continue with the three on, three off rotas as it effects their pay.

Whilst I fully appreciate how this all has affects their ability to pay their bills, it feels as if despite nearly a thousand people dying in the UK today alone, the seriousness of what we are up against right now and the affect it has on us all personally hasn't fully been appreciated. The Trustees are in such a difficult position, it isn't nice being responsible for such decisions. As an employer we are doing all we can to keep our employees safe, which in turn protects the lives of our dogs. We have come so far through this and it has worked. We cannot suddenly make up our own guidelines, we have to follow instructions from the Government.

It does hurt me the fact some of the discontent has been aimed at me personally. No matter what I have done to get us through this, orchestrate and write an appeal that has raised over £20,000 so far, plus a Porsche 911 Cabriolet to raffle. Newspaper coverage, BBC Radio interviews, new protocols at the kennels to make sure that all the dogs are out twice. It feels as if none of it is enough.

The fact is, as a charity we are simply following the Governments guidelines on how to save lives, lives which are very important to SHAK. We are trying to keep the people who make this operation work safe, as well as their families. They are vitally important in our work and greatly appreciated, we are trying to do what is best to keep them safe as well safeguard their jobs.

Jon's words "strong leader" keep coming back to me. Like so many other phrases and memories during this pandemic, they all seem to have another meaning further down the line. I have tried to be a strong leader, sail the ship against the aggressive tides, but I cannot make the weather change and the storms go away. I wish I could. The stress is bubbling away. I am alone, frustrated, angry and burnt out.

Sheba is very much the same, which is good in one way but not so good in another. I am hoping the antibiotics kick in soon, but then I also know they aren't a miracle cure. We lie for a while on the grass when we get home, thinking of how different it would be if it was Easter weekend under normal circumstances.

Despite the evening sun making an appearance as we lie, I still feel empty, alone and completely worn out. Undervalued and taken for granted, or maybe it's the fact it seems as if it hasn't been understood just how much stress, worry and hard work I have done get us this far, hasn't been seen by all. Maybe it is just my time to hit the wall fear and anxiety brings. I too have my own financial worries in all of this, plus my dog is dying. It is all consuming having to live with both and try and help others through their problems. These dogs mean everything to me, but sometimes I wish I just did this on my own.

I cuddle Sheba even tighter and start to cry, my tears wetting the top of her head. I really don't know what else I can do.

Happy Easter.

Day Nineteen.

Saturday 11th April 2020

Total UK Deaths: 917 new deaths, including an 11 year old. Bringing the total of reported deaths to 9,975.

Confirmed Cases: 78,991

- The Queen gives her first ever Easter speech, stating "the coronavirus will not overcome us."
- Police forces from 37 areas have issued 1,084 fines for breaches of coronavirus regulations.
- Spain records its lowest number of coronavirus deaths there in 19 days, suggesting that the outbreak may have peaked. 510 fatalities taking the total to 16,353.

Nothing can satisfy the numbness that I feel right now. There is no medicine which will pacify the pain myself and Rachel feel tonight. There is nothing anyone will say or can do which will heal this hurt.

At 5.30pm we had to say goodbye to the brave little trooper who was our Sheba. I really don't know where to start, or where to end. Everything in this world has gone so mad, the vets are closed, she can't be admitted for fluids or observation. It's me and her, I have to make the decision, there is no alternative with this.

It started with her being a little restless on my bed from about 5am this morning. She didn't seem uncomfortable, we 've enjoyed so many sunrises the last couple of weeks, but today she just couldn't settle.

Then she didn't really want to eat. I cuddled her in her bed in her eating quarters (aka the kitchen as opposed to the utility with the rest of the dogs), her whole body felt so hot. I tried everything which has been successful in the last couple of weeks. Her favourite Butchers tripe loaf, chub rolls, cat food, warm buttery toast. Eventually she settles on four digestive biscuits, just enough I hope, for her to be able to take her antibiotics.

We travel to work like we do on all of my days in, she goes to the toilet outside the kennels and then lies in her bed where she can keep an eye on everyone and everything.

Today is different though, there doesn't seem to be any middle ground. She is either barking and looking a little distressed or sleeping so soundly she doesn't wake when you enter the office. I try to concentrate on work, there are fifty other dogs that need my attention, but I can't help myself from keeping checking on her.

Both myself and Rachel try to get her to eat, again all her favourite things, hot dogs, Bonio biscuits (she went through a full box of them just a couple of days ago) but nothing tempts her.

I walk a few other dogs, knowing exactly what I should do, but I keep putting if off. She might just need to rest. It has been a crazy few days, and today it is so warm.

Dinnertime comes, I get her out for the toilet again and try to feed her, but she still wants nothing. Her body is so hot, and she is beginning to drink excessively. Every living cell in my body sinks. I can't put it off any longer, I text Emily the vet.

The worry and this repetitive world I now exist in, meant I had completely forgotten it was both a Saturday and Easter weekend, she replies saying she isn't at work until Tuesday, but I can take Sheba to her house and she will examine her there. Of course, if the outcome is of the worst possible kind, and I know it will be, she will help Sheba along the way. My mind flashes back to the conversation we had just a couple of days ago. Social distancing means I won't be able to hold her as she dies, I can be there but not with her. My stomach churns at the thought of that, Sheba is very much a typical German Shepherd and is always looking for me. I don't want her to leave us behind frightened because she thinks I am not there. The thought stays with me for the rest of the day.

We finish the day off at the kennels, then I message Emily again to say I really think she has to see her. The pain in typing those words shoots through my body like a knife slicing through butter, but I know our girl is dying. There is a little bit of discharge beginning to appear from her eyes, replacing the sparkle which has been with her during all of this. She looks tired and for the first time since her back legs gave up a few weeks ago, she looks unhappy.

I lift her into the front of the van, she was always such a bad traveller. I don't know whether she had a bad experience being in a vehicle, but she never really settled. She wasn't travel sick or anything like that, she would just bark and be restless. This last journey is no different, only she doesn't have the energy or ability to move around.

I feel physically sick as we drive. One of the worst parts of losing a pet for me, is the drive. All the questions racing around your head, are you really doing the right thing? What if you just turn the van around and go back home? Maybe she will feel better at home. Then there are the last times you are going to do so many things together. Leave the house, put their lead on, hold their head.

It always fills me with dread, this time as we drive down a deserted A1 in glorious sunshine, it is no different. In fact, such surreal surroundings maybe even make it worse. It feels like we are the last two living creatures on this earth, soon it will be only me and I will be left alone.

I pull up at Emily's farmhouse; Rachel arrives behind us in her car just seconds later. She is wearing her sunglasses; I know they mean she has been crying all the way here.

Emily is waiting for us. I tell her everything from two metres away, my voice trembling with every word. Holding back the tears I never take my eyes of Sheba. It's as if I am trying to absorb every single second we have left. Emily just listens, it's so strange not being able to be next to somebody when something so intimate is about to happen.

She has very thoughtfully lain a blanket out under a tree that faces the sun. The birds are singing, and the place looks like an ideal setting for a picnic, peaceful and at this very moment almost magical.

The three of us dance around the blanket, keeping two metres apart as I lift Sheba out of the van and put her down for the last time. She keeps lifting her head to look at me as Emily begins her examination. No wonder her body feels so warm, her temperature is forty, which could mean she is fighting infection. The word pyometra raises its ugly head again. Then there are the mammary tumours that we knew about but only seemed to appear recently. As both are controlled by hormones, Emily thinks that both are probably the cause of what is making Sheba so ill. In normal circumstances x-rays would be taken of her chest to see if the cancer had spread. We obviously can't do such an examination with the present lockdown, we have no choice, the deterioration in her condition in the last twelve hours means we have to let her go.

Emily takes great time to explain everything, how there was nothing we could have done to stop it, having both the cancer and the pyometra means she probably wouldn't have operated even if Sheba had been well enough. Such a huge operation would take such a toll, but the cancer would still be there. She explains the womb infection can be treated with an injection, but as soon as the drugs wear off, it will return. Eventually, she will go into kidney failure and nobody wants such an outcome for their loved one.

We all decide we have to put our own pain to one side and help our girl ease hers. The sun is still shining, and the birds are still singing.

Rachel and I back away and lean against the old stone garden wall. We position ourselves so that Sheba can look straight at us. Her eyes are telling me so much, I tell her I love her and I am so proud I was given the opportunity to have her in my life for nearly two years, when we thought she wouldn't last two days when she arrived.

Emily shaves her leg and begins the end. Sheba keeps looking at me, I tell her she will be ok. I begin to cry and hear Rachel's heart breaking too.

The little dog I have nursed 24 hours a day for the last three weeks or so, lifts her head one last time. She looks at Rachel and me, then turns to look at Emily as if to say, "I'm ready."

Then as she turns her head back to lie on the quilted blanket, she gives me one more look. I can feel the love going in both directions, then she closes her eyes.

Day Twenty.

Sunday 12th April 2020 Easter Sunday

Total UK Deaths: Another 737 have died, taking the total to 10,612

Confirmed Cases: 84,279

- Three more nurses die after testing positive for COVID-19 as the debate about the lack of PPE (Personal Protective Equipment) for NHS workers rages on.
- Boris Johnson is released from hospital but won't return to work immediately. In an interview he states that it "could have gone either way."

This morning I feel empty. Sheba has left a big hole in my life both physically and metaphorically. For weeks now I had a routine which worked around her and the other dogs. From carrying her downstairs, putting her harness on to lift her backend so she could go to the toilet, to hand feeding her. This morning I didn't have to do any of it, the workload severely reduced and it felt strange. I cannot believe she has gone.
 The sun has gone today too. It is cooler and the sky is awash with grey cloud. The beauty of yesterday has disappeared, leaving a drab, mundane feel of another day under lockdown. The feeling engulfs me both inside and out.

The ongoing unhappiness and worry with the shift pattern were still ongoing yesterday, feeling as sensitive and vulnerable as I am right now it almost feels as if I am being hung out to dry.
 Knowing my dog was dying, I cracked big time in the morning.
 Making a call I asked for Joan, Sandra and Jon to deal with it as I simply wasn't in the frame of mind to address any of the information which I was receiving. I felt hurt and angry.

Worn out by everything we were all going through but also by the worry with Sheba, I simple could not take anymore. It is a horrible feeling to admit you are beaten by the pressures of life and can't take anymore, especially when you are as stubborn as I am. Yesterday such an admission was made naturally, not for attention or for effect, I collapsed because I am broken.

I had come to the end of my tether; a feeling of absolute rage took over. With all the talk about money and hours, it felt to me as if the organisation had completely lost the vision of why we exist, a charity that was set up in memory of my very first dog.

Everything was just too much. I was trying to look after Sheba so intensely, I was trying to acknowledge and understand everyone's feelings and worries, but I was also trying to keep everyone safe. I don't have management experience; I have been self-employed for the majority of my working life. The pressure was simply too much. I felt sick and as if the whole world was vibrating around me. My head hurt and my heart was racing. It was always going to flood me at some point, I just could have done without it happening as Sheba was dying.

I think my breakdown was recognised, swiftly a plan of action to combat and put an end to the situation was hatched by the others. Jon decided it was time to accept our offer from a couple of weeks of joining us as a trustee. A meeting with my team and Jon and Sandra was arranged for 1pm, to explain exactly what was happening and what our situation was. Team B also had a meeting scheduled for the same time today.

Our meeting went ok, although it felt very strange listening rather than being the one that was having to do the talking. It gave Collette and Rachel the opportunity to ask any questions they wanted to, whilst giving Jon the chance to lay out in no uncertain terms what was happening. It put everybody in the same position, it made everything clear, it put everyone on the same page.

As I write this, Team B will be having their meeting. I am hoping it helps them in the same way.

It sounds as if the meeting went well. Whilst there are still some serious concerns at the drop in wages for some, I'm led to believe it was understood why. As soon as we are in a position to restore things to how they were we will, we all want things back to normal.

I think the last forty eight hours has confirmed just how much stress and pressure this pandemic has put on everyone. I know how empty and helpless I feel in all this, others must be feeling the same way too. The whole world is being affected; everybody's lives are changing. I cannot see many which are changing for the better. Decisions have to be made I guess, just at times I wish it wasn't me having to make them.

Still, we must all fight on together. If we can continue to work in these small teams, we will survive and get through to the holy rainbow, which is where we all want to be.

I have put my time working from home today to good use by completing another gift aid claim with all the latest donations. The support is still coming in, another cheque for £1,000 arrived yesterday taken the appeal total to £23,239. Such an incredible figure and one beyond my wildest expectations. To everyone who has donated, thank you.

The gift aid claim today is for another £1,656, more than enough to pay another week's wages. That is a relief in itself, just a little bit of pressure released which will allow me to focus on other things.

Day Twenty One.

Monday 13th April 2020
The final day of the original three week lockdown.

Total UK Deaths: 717 taking total to 11,329

Confirmed Cases: 88,621

- Spain begins to loosen lockdown restrictions as daily death tolls continue to drop. Yesterday 517 died, with the lowest daily growth in confirmed cases in over three weeks.
- Italy also records its lowest number of coronavirus deaths in more than three weeks. Plus, for the ninth consecutive day, the number of patients admitted in intensive care or hospital both fell.
- China, however, reports a fresh rise in COVID-19 cases, all along its northern border with Russia. Yesterday it reported 108 new infections, the highest number in 5 weeks and surpassing the 99 recorded on Saturday and more than doubling the 46 from Friday.

This was supposed to be the last entry into this book. Day twenty one, the final day in the Governments proposed three week lockdown. The magical beacon which would show we had been guided home safely across stormy seas by a trusted and sea faring skipper. The truth is we are really no further forward towards seeing the lighthouse shining the way to the white cliffs of safety. I would say we are still very much lost at sea.

In those three weeks we have seen over 10,000 people die within all four corners of the UK, we have seen the Prime Minister himself admitted to intensive care and almost lose his life, we have seen the heir to the throne, Prince Charles, also have to self-isolate after being tested positive for COVID-19, we have seen absolute panic and astonishing ignorance.

Now as the debate starts on if, when or how the Government start to loosen the grip on its restrictions, I really am fearful we are nowhere near ready. This really could be the end of life as we have all known it, no more socialising, no more mixing. The horror film come true, the end of the world, Armageddon.

Sitting in my old Louis chair three weeks ago today and watching history in the making seems such a long time ago, a different world almost. The same can be said for the last time I saw my daughter or family. Relationships have become strained, friendships tested, and the integrity of other citizens has certainly been questioned.

Maybe it's because I live so rurally I haven't seen the country coming together to combat this, the propaganda on the news websites always just shows what it wants you to see, but I don't feel the country is ready to make such a huge and life threatening decision.

I've just returned from my shopping trip to the Co-op in Rothbury. A beautiful little town which would have been a hive of tourists today under any other circumstances. Of course, although you would have no idea by looking at the streets, today is the first bank holiday Monday of the year. A day where everyone feels as if the doom and gloom of the dark winter days is finally over, the start of the summer party season. People start planning summer holidays in the sun, they meet for BBQ's, pubs, clbs and restaurants are rammed for days on end. Winter is dead, long live the summer.

Driving the windy country roads to get there, I pass fields, which despite still needing a little more warmth and sun to photosynthesis to the emerald pastures we all picture, are full of lambs and new life.

They skip and play in little teams, oblivious their stay on this planet will be a short one, whilst their mothers take some time out from parenting and indulge in eating some grass in peace. Ironically, whilst our species is dying all around, another is enjoying the simple things this planet provides.

The side of the roads are also lacking the vibrance of established greenery, but instead to disperse the mundane, there is pockets of intoxicating yellow, as daffodils break the verges in their random manner of disorder. Nobody planted this beautiful and fresh plume of yellow, nature herself dictated their place to grow, helped of course by another of the world's marvellous key workers, the bees.

I smile every time I go past a little clump, feeling a warmth the spring brings and the aforementioned bank holiday Monday, in awe at the work of real heroes. The heater on the Defender though is on full, my padded jacket zipped up to the top. The woolly beanie hat not yet retired for the short months of summer.

I see not another living being until I reach the town itself. No cyclists, no horse riders, no walkers or joggers and not a single other vehicle. There is an eerie feel as I drive slowly through the two fords I need to cross; the water is the only other thing moving. I wonder if it too is deserting me. On the run to something bigger and better, a place where there are no restrictions or rules, everything lives as one in harmony. I wish I could jump in that cold, blue water and float away with it.

In Rothbury itself, I get a feeling of it being the town time forgot. The streams of motorbikes who would normally be parked on the main street as convoys of leather clad bikers stop for refreshments, are simply not there. I can park right outside the door of the supermarket, in fact, I have the choice of at least three spaces. Something which simply never happens. Getting parked is one of the reasons why up until this pandemic broke out, I'd very rarely venture here.

The village green is also awash with the vibrant hue of yellow, reds too as the Tulips join their springtime cousins. The trees add to the rainbow (there's that word again) of natural colour with their pink and white blossoms breaking the backdrop of browns and greys of ancient natural stone. There will be no photo's on social media this year of the blooms of Rothbury on a day trip. The whole town is stagnant and sterile, all that is apart from the Co-op.

I get my shopping which is now just becoming a regular list of the same products. Vegetables to make soup for work, bread for both me and the hens, pasta and rice if there is any available, toilet rolls have become a luxury as far as availability is concerned, and alcohol. I don't think any of us could have gotten this far without alcohol. Even people I have spoken to who aren't normally massive drinkers have raised the point of their increased consumption. Apparently, there was a shortage in tonic water in Alnwick recently, you can imagine the carnage that would have caused.

I drive back over the bridge to head home, past all the dark, empty windows of shops which would normally be illuminated and enticing, but instead of turning left, the way I need to go, I turn right and head towards the river. Subconsciously the thought of drifting away from the troubles guides me. Running water nearly always leads to the sea.

My head has been all over the place the last few days, the thought of sitting in my Land Rover (I have no intention of getting out) and watching the water birds going about their business without a care in the world, appeals to me greatly. If I can clear my head for five minutes, away from the pressures of home, work and life in general, then maybe I can focus on how we positively move everything forward instead of the negativity which has crept into my head and heart.

I slow down to turn into the carpark which I have used so many times to walk the dogs, but I can't enter. Huge, white and red plastic barriers block my path. A huge red sign jumps out at me like a jack in a box, 'CARPARK CLOSED' it says in huge white letters. I have to admit I get a shock at what I have just seen. The news is full of stories of beauty spots being closed, I understand why, but today I need to go here to try and reset myself, to somehow program my body and mind to start again.

'CARPARK CLOSED.'

Like a punch in the face the words hit me. I need to be there; I need to see nature living as if there are no boundaries. I need to see life so I can comprehend I still have one of my own.

'CLOSED'

It takes me a few seconds to comprehend I cannot even do such a simple task as sit and watch the ducks. Then my gaze casts further afield, just to take in a little bit of the surroundings, the big children's play area is also fenced up, this time by the high, grey metal fence panels which surround building sites. No child stands a chance of getting in there, which of course is the intended outcome, but the ugliness of the dull rusty fence against the vibrant colours of the swings, slides and climbing frames is a harsh reminder of everything which is wrong with the world right now. Constrained by a vulgar disease, contained inside by the very same.

 I reverse back out onto the road, looking for a place to turn so I can head home. I continue along until I meet the next entrance on my right, the doctor's surgery. Of course, this car park entrance isn't blocked. I sweep around the parked cars, noticing how few empty parking spaces there are and glancing through the windows as I turn, I see the silhouettes of people busily getting on with their work. I wonder how many people in the building right now will appear in this book as one of the statistics recorded at the end of each day.

My mam sends me a screenshot from Facebook of an appeal by the local shelter who has a destruction policy, stating they have taken in over sixty new animals since the start of the lockdown. It's something I think people are still very ignorant of. At the first sign of financial difficulty the pets are often the first things to go, in some households anyway. You also have the unfortunate pets of the victims of COVID-19. What if they have no relatives who will take over the responsibility of looking after them, what if because people aren't working, they don't have the funds to take on a relatives loved one. Suddenly the most important thing in someone's life is a burden. Unwanted and homeless, the pounds are then perhaps the only option. Rescues such as ours are already struggling to look after the animals we have in our care, it's a horrific situation which has received no thought or help from the Government.

Having worked in that particular pound, I know how high the kill rate can be at times of high pressure. I have been in the room and held the vein for the vet after being tricked with the promise of being promoted to a position where I could make a difference. The promised promotion did not materialise, I have to live with the fact I have played my own guilty part because I felt I had no choice.

Then I realised I did have a choice, I could stop some of the killing, give an option to the body bag, that is why I formed SHAK.

I wonder how many of those sixty plus animals will come to their deaths in the very same room. I wonder how many will find new homes once this is all over with. My heart sinks with the thought. Another day ends in tears, frustration and desperation. When will this all end?

Day Twenty Two.

Tuesday 14th April 2020

Total UK Deaths: Hospital deaths 778, taking the total to 12,107

Confirmed Cases: 93,873

-
- Figures are beginning to emerge which will show a huge rise in the UK death toll, as none of the figures so far include people who have lost their lives in care homes, hospices etc. The total the Government have been announcing daily have been the deaths in hospitals only. Patients who have tested positive for COVID-19 before saying goodbye to this world.

So, we now start the unofficial period of lockdown where nobody has a shimmer of light in mind, nobody knows when this is going to end. We have nothing to give us hope or look forward to. According to reports the Government are having a meeting on Thursday to discuss reducing the restrictions, ludicrous to even think about it at this point in my very humble opinion. The fact above about not even having a true figure on the death toll, shows just how little anyone knows about this virus, or what there is still to come from it. It also indicates the Government have been pulling the wool over our eyes the whole time. What else have they been keeping secret?

It's certainly a very strange situation and the world we are all now living in is one of uncertainty and death.

An old girlfriend of mine died on the 2nd April from breast cancer. We were together in our late teens for five years. Just kids trying to be adults really. Today is her funeral, only ten close family members including her husband are allowed at the service. It shows just how sheltered our lives have become, how small. Not being able to give her the send-off she deserved must be terrible for her family and friends, not being able to mourn properly will deny closure. She was only 45.

From my sitting room window, I am lucky enough to have a great view of the Simonside hills which are the huge expanse just before you arrive at Rothbury. Last night there was a mass of black smoke rising from the hills after an accident involving burning the heather. I don't believe anyone was injured, although I'm sure wildlife will have suffered. There was something quite apocalyptic in watching the smoke battle with the sunset for supremacy. Reds, pinks and yellows consumed by dark grey and black. All the colours of the rainbow smothered by the darkness of a stronger and more evil force. It felt like I was watching another piece of misery and death right before my eyes.

Nature again was on her back foot, fighting against a manmade disaster. I sat and watched till eventually the firefighters must have gotten the blaze under control, as the dark descended everything just became black.

Day Twenty Three.

Wednesday 15th April 2020

UK Hospital Deaths: 761 taking the total to 12,868

Confirmed Cases: 98,476

- The Government announces a package of measures to try and stop the spread of coronavirus in care homes. These include improved access to PPE. A crisis is looming due to the deaths in such establishments not being registered on the government's official figures.
- Connie Titchen is released from hospital having recovered from coronavirus. At 106 she thought to be the UK's oldest survivor of the virus.
- UK Police have dished out 3,203 fines to people for allegedly breaching lockdown rules, in just over two weeks.
- People urged to stop using sky lanterns as part of the weekly tribute to NHS workers because of the serious danger they pose to livestock and wildlife.
- High street companies Oasis and Warehouse both enter administration, with 200 people losing their jobs immediately and 1800 placed on furlough as a buyer is sought.
- A pharmacist is arrested during an investigation into the illegal sale of coronavirus testing kits.

The sun has been shining from the moment I opened my eyes, up to me sitting with a well-deserved cold beer and writing this. The weather has been simply glorious today, unlike some of the headlines above.

On a day when so much negativity hogs the headlines, it was great to just get the dogs out into the sunshine and have some fun. Little Major particularly seemed in good spirits, with all his problems with his back end, we obviously have no idea what difference some warmth and a bit of vitamin D can make.

On the way to work, the radio was just full of fury at the lack of PPE, with politicians, care home workers, council staff all stating the obvious problems and blaming the government. One even went as far as calling it a national disgrace. I don't know what the answer is to all of this, but I do think there will be a fall out at some point as questions are asked of the Conservative's response to such a dramatic situation.

Anyway, there is nothing I can do about it, it is all out of my control. I did not vote this Government into power; they do not care about the thoughts of people like me. I try to remain positive, clinging desperately to the chemicals in my brain which the sunshine has produced and stimulated. It has been such a beautiful day.

With everything which has been going on lately, it was nice just to be able to put our hearts and souls into making the most of the sun with the dogs. Amazing how a feeling of summer can lift the spirits.

Today we hit fifty six consecutive days the dogs have all been outside twice. Given the limited hands on, it is something we should all be proud of.

Day Twenty Four.

Thursday 16th April 2020

UK Hospital Deaths: 861 taking total to 13,729

Confirmed Cases: 103,093

- Boris Jonson's stand in, Dominic Raab announces the current lockdown restrictions will continue for at least another three weeks, taking us up until the 7th May. This falls in line with comments made by the Prime Minister on 19th March that the UK could take twelve weeks to "turn the tide" on coronavirus.
- Captain Tom Moore, aged 99, raises over £14,000,000 for the NHS after his challenge of walking a hundred laps of his garden goes viral. There are now calls for him to be knighted.
- In Spain, some cemeteries are hosting six funerals per hour, such is the horrific impact of the coronavirus.
- Figures announce there were more than 1,600 deaths in England and Wales which were outside hospitals and linked to COVID-19 in March alone. An alarming figure which illustrates the UK's death toll maybe way higher than is being reported.
- Mary Agyeiwaa Agyapong, a 28 year old nurse who was heavily pregnant, dies from coronavirus. Her baby is successfully delivered by caesarean and is reported to be doing well.

At last the Government give some clarification of what is happening, by officially extending the lockdown for another three weeks. There has been so much uncertainty surrounding the last couple of days, with people unsure of what is going on and when this is going to end. At least now we know that until the 7th of May everything stays the same. Game on.

At the kennels, things are just continuing as normal. Every day is beginning to blend into one, despite the fact so much is put into making the day as enjoyable for the dogs as we can. Routine breeds complacency but I am determined we will come out of this stronger than ever before. If not, what is the point of going on and working ourselves to beyond exhaustion now?

I have started making little lists for when this is over. Nothing majorly important, but things like which dogs are gaining weight from the reduced exercise, which one's condition has deteriorated a little due to not having the time to groom them as much as we did, and the ones who are maybe showing signs of age and wear and tear. I have already arranged with Emily for a vet's visit once this is done, we have already discussed x-rays for Merlin and his limp for example, whilst at the moment he will continue getting pain relief.

All just things which need looked at, things which would normally be addressed, but our hands are tied whilst everywhere is shut. We can just do the best we can for now.

Behind the scenes there was a bit of good news this afternoon, when the council informed Jon he had been successful in his application for a grant to compensate for the lack of trading from our shop in Blyth. It seems such a long time ago the shop was the hub of our fundraising and a hive of activity. It had really just fully established itself, then this all kicked off, so a grant of £10,000 is a huge help.

It also represents the first piece of help the charity has received from the Government during this crisis. A lot of people seem to presume because we are a charity, we are receiving grants from all over the place. The harsh truth is because we deal with animal welfare rather than people, we receive very little. We are on our own and have our future in our own hands to some extent, but an added bonus like today's news really does lift some of the unseen worry.

Day Twenty Five.

Friday 17th April 2020

UK Hospital Deaths: 847 making a total of 14,576

Confirmed Cases: 108,692

- 99 year old Captain Tom Moore has now raised over £20,000,000 for the NHS by walking 100 laps of his garden.
- Britain must be prepared for further waves of coronavirus says leading physician Professor Anthony Costello. The Professor says the country must face up to the "harsh reality" it did not react quickly enough to the pandemic. Suggesting the UK could end up with the highest coronavirus death rate in Europe, whilst there could be as many as six waves of the virus within the next twelve months.
- The Government launches a taskforce to help produce a vaccine for coronavirus with deputy chief medical officer Jonathan Van Tam heading it up.
- The now standard Thursday Clap for Carers causes a stir in London as Metropolitan Police Officers receive heavy criticism for allowing people to breach social distancing rules whilst clapping on Westminster Bridge. Footage from last night shows people standing next to each other, with no following of the two metre guideline.

The success of Captain Tom Moore's garden walks has been nothing short of magnificent, congratulations to him for raising such an unimaginable amount of money.

However, it has certainly made me think about how we can continue to safeguard the lives of our dogs by keeping the charity going. The existing appeal which I set up nearly a month ago is still bringing in money. Yes, the constant flow of PayPal notifications has dried up, but cheques and the odd online payment still arrive.

The total currently stands at £23,454. An absolutely incredible figure for something which was launched out of desperation in a time when everyone is struggling to survive themselves. Thank you to everybody who has contributed, it really does mean the difference between life and death for the charity and the dogs.

The worry is though this pandemic could go on for months yet. The longer it runs, the more people may lose their jobs, the less disposable income they will have. Despite being a vast amount of money to us, what we have now will not last forever. I need to come up with a new and unique method of keeping us in people's thoughts.

The charity has always appreciated every penny which is donated, because I can remember when I started it all and had to suffer things like sponsored chest waxes to raise enough money to pay our kennels bill. In those days it cost us £5 per day per dog. Even if we only had maybe six in our care, that was £30 per day. That in turn was £210 per week, £840 per month. You can see how the numbers added up, and I only had so many hairs on my chest!

Every donation has therefore always meant so much. The total in this current appeal is just something which I would have never thought possible. So where do I go to keep driving the campaign.

I did a draft this afternoon of a little story, told by an anonymous dog in our kennels. The idea is to try and understand how the dogs must be feeling. Whilst they have adapted to the new routine very well, they must be missing the extra social interaction and exercise. Maybe if I can describe the impact the effect of all of this has had on them, but from their point of view, it might hit home.

It's a bit of a challenge, and one I will be working on over the next day or two, as it needs to be right. It needs to work.

My first ever book, It's A Dog's Life, seemed to be well received by people. Describing experiences and telling stories of dogs in a pound, through the eyes of a stray Rottweiler, I often get compliments on how the book made people think, and cry! I need to get my head back in that place and write something along those lines.

Day Twenty Six.

Saturday 18th April

UK Hospital Deaths: 888 taking total to 15,464

Confirmed Cases: 114,217

- The number of fatalities in Spain has increased by another 565 taking the total to 20,043. Currently, only the United States and Italy have lost more of their people.
- The UK now has the fifth highest fatality rate in the world from COVID-19
- Over 150,000 people worldwide have lost their lives.
- At least 50 NHS workers have now died from the disease.
- Councils to be given an extra £1.6 billion funding to help deal with the coronavirus crisis.
- Captain Tom Moore knocks Dame Vera Lynn off the number one spot on the iTunes chart after recording a version of You'll Never Walk Alone with Michael Ball and the NHS Voices for Care Choir.

COVID-19 From Our Dogs Point Of View by Stephen Wylie.

"Nobody comes to see us anymore. I don't know why, there used to be so many people and we used to have such good fun.

Everyday there was some one different who would come in and take us out. We never knew who it would be, but that just added to the excitement. All of us in here used to love it when they came.

Some brought cooked meat and other goodies, some took us away in their car to the seaside, others would just play with the ball with us until we were exhausted.

People still come in to see us, but it's the same ones. They work so hard for a few days, but they have all the boring stuff to do as well, like the cleaning. It takes until dinnertime because there is so few of them. Every day is the same, then they disappear too. Replaced by another three that work just as hard.

I heard one of them talking about a virus yesterday and how people aren't allowed out of their houses anymore. But I can't believe that. All that time ago when I had a house to live in, my person would be out all of the time. Sometimes they'd leave me there alone all day or night.

It must be like being stuck in this kennel forever, I couldn't imagine that. No seaside, no fields, no ball! Poor people how are they expected to live their lives like that? I love going out.

This virus kills people if they get too close apparently, something to do with touching each other. What if they don't want to touch us anymore? Will that mean we won't get any cuddles? Or a pat on the head when we bring the ball back? I love it when they do that to me. It makes me feel happy that I have made them happy.

What happens if all the people die? Every single one that comes here to see us. Who will feed and walk us then? We will end up trapped inside forever like they are now.

We still get out twice a day at the moment. Once to sunbathe in the back run with a tasty treat and once for our walk around the field, it's a bit shorter but we still get to smell all the smells and look at the lambs who are even more curious and playful than us.

We get our tummies filled twice too, which is one of the best parts of the day, but it just isn't the same as it has to be done so quickly. The people seem to be under so much pressure.

One of them was talking about what they would do if things run out this morning. Laundry liquid, whatever that is, and fleece blankets. Apparently, we go through so many of them. I love curling up in those blankets, but the dog in the next kennel sometimes rips them when he gets bored.

Apparently with nobody being allowed to go out to the shops, people aren't able to donate and keep our supplies topped up. The person said he was worried that one day we might run out completely. That made me worry too, I really don't want to sleep on just a cold concrete floor.

Life here has never been perfect, how could it be without a sofa to sleep on, a fire to lie in front of, or a family to call my very own, but it was as close as it could be. We had company and nice things, we got attention and love. Some of us in here had never had any of that before

The man said they would do all they could to make sure we still have them, and that things would go to back to normal soon, but I could see the worry in his eyes.

I am worried and anxious too. I want things to be how they used to be and still don't understand why everything has changed."

The appeal we have been running so far has been an incredible success. We have seen such fantastic support for something which was launched out of desperation in a time when everyone is struggling. Thank you to everybody who has contributed, it really does mean the difference between life and death.

The worry is though this pandemic could go on for months yet. The longer it runs, the more people may lose their jobs, the less disposable income they will have. Despite being a vast amount of money to us, what we have now will not last forever.

We have started to have to buy the things that you usually so very kindly donate, because you can no longer get out to the shops. Things like laundry liquid, bin bags, dog waste bags. They all now need bought, which in turn eats into the funds that we have.

Bedding supplies too are going down, as people can't get out and about to donate them in the shop or the donation bins. Soon we may even have to start buying the fleece blankets that all the dogs like, spending more money.

I have to stress that we are NOT at a crisis point yet, careful planning and trying to stay one step ahead has gotten us this far through the COVID-19 pandemic. I am simply trying to stay that step ahead. The dog's future really does depend on it.

I know things are especially tight for everybody right now, but if you can spare a little, you can make a donation via PayPal:

paypal.me/shaksanctuary

Or by sending a cheque (made payable to SHAK) to SHAK. Greenwell Road, Alnwick, Northumberland. NE66 1HB.

You can order the products we use in the safety of your home from our Amazon Wishlist:

https://www.amazon.co.uk/hz/wishlist/ls/378KO9YKHAI9D?ref_=wl_share

Or when you do venture out for your shopping maybe you can also drop bedding donations (no pillows or duvets please for storage and disposal) and other things in our donation bins at Sainsburys Alnwick (food only), Pets At Home Alnwick (they've kindly agreed to accept anything), or outside our HQ in Greenwell Road Alnwick.

Unfortunately, we are also governed by the rules of lockdown and are unable to collect any donations apart from our designated drop off points.

The support from all of you has been magnificent. It has given us the courage and faith to go on, even in the most difficult of times. We wouldn't still be here without it, without you. But as this awful time goes on and on, we will need you even more.

Thank you so much and stay safe.

Stephen Wylie
Founder of SHAK & Author of It's A Dogs Life.

So that is it. An afternoons work trying to keep the momentum going of an appeal which could make sure we are still here in however many months' time when this is finally all over.
    I enjoyed going back in time and entering a dogs head again, I hope you have enjoyed reading it just as much.

Day Twenty Seven.

Sunday 19th April 2020

UK Hospital Deaths: 596 (the smallest increase in almost two weeks) taking the total number of deaths to 16,060

Confirmed Cases: 120,067

- The Education Secretary announces there is no date set for schools to return.
- A plane loaded with 68 tonnes of PPE arrives from China and is already on its way to the frontline.
- Doctors and nurses clap as the first two patients from London's Nightingale hospital are discharged to continue their recuperation in a standard hospital.
- Belgium become the latest European country to begin lifting restrictions.
- The Government has announced they are going to give free laptops and tablets to children with disadvantaged backgrounds to help study at home during lockdown.
- Spain to continue lockdown but will reduce restrictions for children.

It is a beautiful morning today, sunshine, blue skies and very little wind. A perfect day for gardening.

First though, I go through my usual checks of emails and look to see if we have received any new donations. The update I wrote yesterday seems to have been well received, with plenty of messages saying it had people in tears. As harsh as it sounds, it means it had the desired effect, I wanted people to fully understand just what is at stake here, but also for people to try and help us even more.

It seems to have worked on both levels, as within the first 24 hours there was an influx of £375. Perhaps slightly more important just now, we also had several offers of bedding. Such a simple thing, but with collection arranged, it means a crisis which was perhaps a week away with supplies running low, has now been avoided.

It has spurred others on too. Volunteer Mick has set up a 5k challenge run/walk on Facebook to help raise funds, which it has immediately, whilst the work of Charlotte, Mike, Brad and Amy cannot be underestimated as the eBay page continues to thrive.

Such amazing support from everybody, when we get through this, I hope everyone is as proud of their efforts as I am. I sent the last two updates to Radio Newcastle host Alfie Joey, my contact who invited me to talk on the show a couple of weeks back. His response to them was great, he especially seemed to like the latest one, COVID-19 From One Of Our Dogs Point Of View.

"That is brilliantly written. May get some of it voiced up." Was his comeback. I'm not entirely sure what it means, but hopefully it may lead to a little bit more press coverage and keep our plight in the public eye.

Day Twenty Eight.

Monday 20th April 2020

UK Hospital Deaths: 449 (another decline from yesterday) with the total now standing at 16,509

Confirmed Cases: 124,743

- The UK's Furlough scheme began at 7am this morning, a new online portal that should reimburse companies with 80% of employee's wages whilst they have been on 'gardening leave' during this crisis. It is believed two thirds of firms have furloughed some staff. By 4pm today over 140,000 firms had applied for the scheme, hoping to receive grants to pay the wages of over a million people.
- The delayed flight from Turkey carrying 84 tonnes of PPE, which was due to land yesterday alongside the one from China, is expected to arrive today.
- A minute's silence in memory of all the key workers who have died from COVID-19 is to be held at 11am on the 28th April. The plan hatched by Unison, the Royal College of Nursing and the Royal College of Midwives are asking for the whole nation to join in.
- Rioting reported in Paris as tensions escalate over the coronavirus lockdown.
- The UK reveal plans to create another 30,000 mortuary spaces for victims of COVID-19.
- In the USA oil prices plunge below zero for the first time in history, as traders stop buying because of the coronavirus pandemic.

I don't know if it is just me, but there seems to be a resignation in our existence now. I think everyone expected the extension to lockdown, so it really came as no surprise last Thursday, but a month on from the original statement from Boris Johnson I wonder where all this is going.

My life has changed beyond recognition, as I'm sure everybody else's has, but living in this void no longer makes me sad or happy. I just exist.

The routine we have had to bring into the kennels to keep everyone safe, means there is no weekly structure. Every day is one of two exact same protocols. Work or home.

There is still an underlying current of discontentment at the reduced hours for some, and understandably so, but we are fighting against an invisible killer which shows no mercy to anyone, no matter who you are, the Trustee's had to make the call to help protect the lives of all our loved ones.

So, with that in mind, my life has descended into two different days, each of which repeat themselves three times before giving in and letting the other world take over.

I am neither bored nor exhausted, it is just the way it is. A bit like Groundhog Day, only it all revolves every three days. The only parts of the world I have seen in a month are the kennels, the Co-op in Rothbury and home. The only people I have encountered long enough to have any interaction or conversation with face to face is Rachel and Collette. No daughter, no family, nothing. Even those days when I nursed Sheba to the very end seem such a long time ago. They say time heals, but at the moment the mundane drudgery is doing nothing but numbing the pain for further down the line. I miss her so much.

I have done more gardening at home in the last month, than I have in the five and a half years I have lived here. Yet, there is still so much to do. Three days cuts things short, it's not enough. In the previous world the kind of work I've been getting through would have been stretched out and extended during a week's holiday.

The sun has decided to show now too, meaning the dark and wet days which seemed to last forever are fading into a memory. Not right back into the distance yet, but like when the sky begins to clear after a storm, those thunderous clouds are making their way out to sea.

    I see jobs all over the house which haven't been done. Walls which need painting, but I am not allowed out to buy paint, rooms need decorated, but I couldn't find the wallpaper I wanted before lockdown. Every day I look at them and the scuff marks which come with wear and tear of owning dogs, but I do nothing about it. I started to look online when this all kicked off, but how can you judge colours from a picture on your mobile phone? In the end I have just given up.

At the kennels we were just beginning to make huge progress with repairs, modernisation and changes. They too have been put on hold. Piles of rubble and soil, polluted by debris which has resurfaced after years of lying under weeds and stringy unkept grass, sit on the unfinished car parking area like some ancient burial mound. Every time I look at them, I feel a little tinge of sadness at how close we were to making the changes we have wanted to for years.

    I know the builders will be back, they have done so much for us and have such belief in our work, but what if they are too busy trying to save their own businesses to donate their very valuable time and expertise to us for free?

    In all of this of course, the one thing that matters the most is the dogs, not painting my kitchen. The whole reason my life has gone through this change is to protect them.

    I just feel flat today and have done for the last couple of days. Not down, not depressed, just as if this is how it might be forever.

    There is light at the end of the tunnel, we will all come through this, the rainbow which keeps being mentioned and which I see in more and more windows when I leave the sanctuary of the house, will cast its glorious arc over each and every one of us.

    But like those deep, dark storm clouds which are now making their unwelcome appearance on somebody else's shores, the majestic and beautiful collection of reds, yellows and blues seem so far away.

Day Twenty Nine.

Tuesday 21st April 2020

UK Hospital Deaths: 823 taking the total to 17,337

Confirmed Cases: 129,044

- UK vaccine for coronavirus will begin being used on humans from Thursday, Health Secretary Matt Hancock has revealed in the Governments daily briefing. Developed by scientists at the University of Oxford, they say it has an 80% chance of success.
- The number of deaths from COVID-19 in care homes have more than quadrupled in a week, from 217 to 1043.
- Scientists in China have discovered more than 30 mutations of the coronavirus, which they say may explain why it has had such a devastating effect in different parts of the world.
- Charlene Merrifield was arrested in Hebburn, after a report a woman had attempted to attack a man with a knife. The 39 year old was today jailed for more than four months after she deliberately coughed at a police officer.
- Oil prices hit the lowest level in 21 years after the collapse in market of US crude oil.

First day back of three in and it is always a strange feeling. I am so used to being here most of the time, after time off I feel guilty about leaving the dogs. I always scrutinise everyone when I get them out for the rest of the team to clean, not because I don't trust the people on the other shift, just because it has always been the way. I am responsible for them; it was me who agreed that they could come and spend their days here when they needed somewhere to go the most. I think of them all as I would my own dogs.

Casper came to us the day he was due to be destroyed by another rescue. He had bitten several handlers, but the day before the bite his behaviour was a little bit worse. His problem seems to stem from his life previous to rescue, where it was said he was used in dog fighting. Being a Staffordshire Bull Terrier, the training these idiots use to strengthen the dogs jaw muscles, includes hanging them by the mouth from trees.

The bite incidents involving Casper all follow the same pattern, he would lunge at the tree at the far end of the paddock he would go into on his walks. Once he couldn't hang on to the branches, he would redirect at anything else he could take in his mouth. It didn't matter whether it was somebody's arm or leg. He just had a need to bite and hang on to something.

It was during the time he had been abused in this way; he had broken his front left leg. Judging by the physical state of the elbow, he wasn't taken to the vets. The damage was left to heal itself which it has done so horrendously.

Despite the pain and the joint being swollen and disfigured, he manages extremely well to get around as normal, but x-rays showed a lot of arthritic change.

Obviously in later life, this is going to cause him problems. So, it was decided by the vet and the other rescue to amputate the leg whilst he was young enough to adapt. His appointment was made for what turned out to be the day after his latest bite. Which in turn was changed to an appointment to be destroyed. As an afterthought, I received a phone call to ask if I would go to the kennels and assess him. I was the only hope he had of his life being saved.

The dog I saw running around the paddock looked just like any other white Staffy who loved his life regardless. He was sniffing everywhere, exploring and leaving his mark. Not once did he attempt to attach himself to the tree, he had no interest in biting me. How could I send this dog to his death when all he had done wrong was exactly what he had been trained to do?

I put him in my van and took him with me. He had been less than 24 hours from losing a limb, then his very existence. I was hopeful his life could actually start now.

Once at my kennels, I gave him something to do and perhaps more importantly something to carry in his mouth. My idea was if his mouth was already full, then he wouldn't want to latch onto anything else. From the very first day he arrived he has carried his training dummy everywhere. He has not bitten since the last incident in his previous rescue.

We had his leg checked out by Emily and the x-rays were sent over to her. She confirmed the arthritis was quite bad, but we both agreed this little dog had enough to get over without giving him the obstacle of adapting to three legs. A plan of pain relief and monitoring was hatched. Despite his disfigurement he is still a little tank on the lead, I'd go as far as saying he doesn't even realise he has the problem.

So, today I got him out for his morning walk and noticed the joint was heavily swollen to how it was three days previous. He wasn't walking any different, still pulling like a train, but through the fur the joint looked inflamed and the skin was red.

I took photographs and sent them to Emily. She remembered Casper from his last examination and during this lockdown photos and videos are all the vets can really go on. She thought it could just be a flare up with his arthritis, and to introduce pardale into his medication, a paracetamol based drug which might help.

Casper is a dog I have always felt for. His life so far has been a succession of everything bad. He doesn't know the things we take for granted for our own pets. He has never felt the love and affection which would make him relax enough so he didn't need to carry his dummy. Now though, he has somewhere which believes he can be turned around, perhaps more importantly he is with people who believe in him. That is a good place to start.

Away from the kennels we are starting to see the physical benefits of the update that I posted a few days ago. The Amazon van drivers must be sick of coming to my house to deliver parcels, as the last couple of days has seen an amazing response. Boxes of fleece blankets, laundry liquid, bin liners, coconut oil, treats and kennel disinfectant have all arrived in abundance thanks to peoples amazing generosity.

I've said it before but knowing people are behind us and want us to continue to be able to give our dogs the best, means so much to us. It gives me motivation to keep putting out the appeals and updates, it drives me on to continue with this writing project, so you can all see for yourselves how important your support is.

Without all of this and the valuable service the Amazon drivers provide, we would have been in a terrible state. I know some people have mixed views on Amazon but having everything available and delivered to the door has been essential in our survival. As far as key workers go, the driver's contribution to keeping us and the whole country running should be recognised when all of this is over.

Day Thirty.

Wednesday 22nd April 2020

UK Hospital Deaths: 763 taking the total to 18,100

Confirmed Cases: 133,495

- Health Secretary Matt Hancock claims the UK is now at the peak of the coronavirus outbreak in the House of Commons, as the total of hospital deaths tops 18,000
- Whilst the death toll seems to have "flattened off" there will be "no sudden fall away" in cases, Chris Whitty (England's chief medical officer) has said.
- An urgent appeal has been issued by the teams at the University of Oxford and Imperial College London, for volunteers to take part in human trials for a potential coronavirus vaccine. With a bounty offered up to £625 to those who take part.
- Stephen Hawking's family donate his ventilator to the Royal Papworth Hospital in Cambridge.
- Spain announce plans to ease lockdown restrictions in the second half of May but warns restrictions could return if cases begin to rise again.
- The US State of Missouri is suing China after 200 people die from coronavirus, for "enormous death, suffering and economic loss."
- Six dogs are being trained to detect for coronavirus in passengers arriving at UK airports. Norman, Digby, Storm, Star, Jasper and Asher a mix of Spaniels, Labradors and a Labradoodle, will all go through training by the Medical Detection Dogs charity at a cost of £500,000.
- The first load of PPE ordered from Turkey arrives in the UK, as it emerges that the company supplying it did not have enough stock to fulfil the order.

- Brandon Wallace (21) is jailed for six months after claiming he had coronavirus and spitting at two Police officers, whilst being arrested for domestic assault.
-

When the lockdown came into place, it was amazing how many people suddenly started enquiring about getting a dog. Whilst I could understand the reasons behind this, all the time at home etc, it just didn't sit comfortable with me.

To me, it's like rehoming a dog near Christmas. A completely alien time to everyday life, a period which is far removed the everyday routines and habits of a family thus I just don't feel it is fair to put a dog in a home just now.

For example, the parents aren't at work, the children aren't at school, neither have any form of routine. What happens when the time comes for circumstances to change? Even worse, what happens if the parents lose their jobs and suddenly months down the line the finances aren't there to commit to another mouth to feed? Worse still, what happens it the new owner catches this dreadful infection and is then unable to look after the dog.

Logistically too, there are issues. The way we have always rehomed in the past has included a number of visits which start with a home interview, before the potential new owner meets the dog at the kennels for the first time.

These meetings get more and more intense and progress into trip's away in the car, to the beach for example, then reach the point when the dog makes an appearance in the home. Sometimes there are even sleep overs or weekend stays. The idea behind all of this is so when the time comes to make the move permanently, nothing is new. It has been in and out of the car, it has met the neighbours, it knows exactly where its bed is.

We will not take risks or compromise on this; the dogs have been messed about enough. Trying to orchestrate all of these things whilst the whole country is in complete lockdown is just not feasible.

There is, however, always an exception to the rule. Regular followers of the charity will remember in the winter of 2019 we made an appeal to get some of the older dogs into homes to protect their old bones from the aches and pains the cold of winter brings on.

One wonderful lady applied, living alone she wasn't bothered what the dog looked like or what breed it was, she just wanted the company and to help a dog find warmth.

Dot is close friends of our volunteers Mick and Lesley. Her health isn't as it used to be, but for a dog who wants to potter about in the garden and enjoy the sea air, it is an ideal home.

Between us, we all decided it was a perfect opportunity for Sally, an old American Bulldog who had been with us for a few years but was beginning to show her age. Her hearing was very poor, and she was displaying a lack of interest in walking the field. Thinking of her seeing out her time in kennels when she was showing signs of becoming unhappy wasn't an option.
Sally had a great last few months with Dot, being spoilt and living a simple and relaxing life. She showed us all her loving side and enjoyed the affection and attention of a woman who simply adored her. It was the perfect match.

Unfortunately, one thing we can't compete against is cancer, such a devastating and vicious disease. We all had to say goodbye to Sally at the vets together after she had become ill. Scans showed she was riddled with tumours which probably explained the deterioration in her passion for life at the kennels. There was nothing we could do. Dot was devasted but knew she had given Sally the best days of her life. Knowing so meant the world to her.

This week Dot decided she was ready to do the same all over again and offer one of our oldies a seaside retreat to soak in the sun. I spoke to Mick and offered up three candidates, Hobo, Bully and Barney.

All three are old boys with a bit of a chequered past, but all three have grown older, wiser and turned into such characters.

It was a hard one to call, but Mick felt Barney would be better suited to what Dot could offer. I trusted his judgement.

Keeping to the social distancing guidelines and not setting a foot in the kennels, Mick arrived ready to escort Barney to his new home. I got him out and lifted him into the boot of his car. Barney was excited but nervous too. It was clear he wasn't sure what was happening.

Barney's story is a really sad one. Arriving with us after being found as a stray in the Sheffield area. He was so independent, ignorant and strong, nobody had reclaimed him or looked to offer him a home. Such is the world in these pounds, he was booked into be destroyed. Which was when I got the usual phone call.

He'd clearly had no input into his manners or shown any affection and being an Akita cross German Shepherd, it certainly didn't help with the stubbornness.

Deep down though you could see there was a loving boy in there, behind all the brashness and power. He was probably only about two years old.

We found him a home with a wonderful family who fell in love with him the minute they saw him. It was quickly decided he was the one for them. They idolised Barney and worked so hard at his issues with strangers and other dogs, both of which just seemed to escalate. Sticking by him during the thick and the thin, love grew stronger and stronger.

Then one day an accident happened which wasn't Barneys fault and unfortunately, he lost his home and his family, meaning he had to come back to us. All because somebody wouldn't listen when they were asked to leave him be.

His family were broken to the point they have never had another dog since, such was their love for Barney. They still keep in touch and make donations towards his up-keep, the regret of what happened to him never easing. The return has been as hard for them as it was for Barney.

His size, stubbornness and now his history has constantly gone against him, also the fact that he is neither an Akita nor a German Shepherd. Both are such intelligent breeds but are also so head strong and opiniated I find it is always a demanding mix. We had a wonderful dog called Lennox who was the same cross. He was very hard work to begin with but eventually he got there, living with me for 8 years. We lost him last year at the age of sixteen, he was one of the best I've ever known.

Fast forwarding again to today, receiving photographs of Barney looking somewhat confused but happy in Dot's sitting room and garden means a lot to us. Especially in such a strange and difficult time.

We all know Dot and we know the home. I am under no illusions about what is on offer for Barney, nor the pace of life he will have. Just like Sally before him, he will want for nothing and receive as much love as he wants. I think in time the favour will be returned to Dot; he just needs to realise how fortunate he is. Barney is clever, it hopefully won't take him long.

It's been another busy day for the Amazon drivers as more parcels arrive. It is all simply amazing.

Collette and Rachel have worked really hard at the kennels, and between the three of us we manage to treat every dog for fleas and ticks. Quite an achievement considering the work already involved in looking after the fifty dogs we have. There are a few which I thought would react to such an invasion of their privacy, but only two do. Zeus has a growl to tell me he has had enough, Benji snaps his teeth at a similar point.

I laugh it off though, if only they knew how hard we were all trying to keep things as normal as possible.

Day Thirty One.

Thursday 23rd April 2020

UK Hospital Deaths: 616 taking the total to 18,738. The lowest weekday increase since 2nd April.

Confirmed Cases: 138,078

- Essential workers and their households will be able to book tests for coronavirus online from tomorrow, the Health Secretary Matt Hancock has said in the Governments daily briefing.
- B&Q reopen half of its UK stores, joining a number of companies trying to get back to work despite the government lockdown.

After all the drama, arguments, worries, stress, meltdowns and anxieties over the last thirty days, today was one that we all simply worked hard and enjoyed the sunshine with the dogs.

With the handover to Rich, Sarah and Catherine at the end of our shift, we had a little team meeting in the morning and outlined the jobs which needed done before we left. We also looked at the jobs which had maybe been a little overlooked because of the pressure which comes with only three being in.

For example, Collette gave the back kennels which have been vital in our operation over the last month, a really good clean, Rachel emptied all the 'drain buckets' and bleached them, whilst I did a little war dance in the skip which contains all the bags of dog waste to create as much space as possible.

The skip is nearly full, and I have ordered a replacement, another £300 spent, so it is vital we can fit in as much rubbish as possible. The heat and sun made the job even more 'sludgy' and I found the aroma even more over whelming, but it gave me some sort of sense of achievement and normality!

On the way home we call by Emily's house to pick up medication for the dogs and Sheba's ashes. The bag left on the other side of the same garden wall we leant against not that long ago, whilst Emily talks to us front her back doorstep.

In the past I have always felt when a dog I have loved so much returns home it gives closure. Such are the circumstances right now I don't think anything can offer closure. It is all so surreal and almost dream like. As a child I used to pretend I was the only person left on earth if I couldn't sleep. I'd try and figure out how I'd cope and what it would be like. Usually because my mind was taken away from the issue of being unable to sleep, I'd drift off within minutes.

This is the nearest I've ever felt to those role plays. Nothing is normal and everything seems like it's happening in a different lifetime.

Sheba is home, but sometimes it feels like she has never left. Then, other times it almost feels like she was never here.
Of course, I have all the memories, but with the ambience of seeing no one or going anywhere, time itself seems to have lost its structure and purpose.

Day Thirty Two.

Friday 24th April 2020

UK Hospital Deaths: 684 taking the total to 19,506

Confirmed Cases: 143,464

- New online system for ordering coronavirus test applications has temporarily closed after 5,000 home kits were ordered in just two minutes.
- Metropolitan Police announce there have been 4,000 domestic abuse arrests in London in the last six weeks.
- Matt Hancock states it is too soon to end lockdown, but he is happy some businesses are beginning to reopen their doors.
- Doctors at Warrington Hospital in Cheshire have cut mortality rates and improved recovery times from COVID-19 by adapting machines which are usually used to help breathing in a sleeping disorder.

Back on my own self-induced isolation today as my three days away from the kennels commence with gorgeous sunshine. At last it feels as if we are beginning to move out of the darkness.

Mick pays Barney a visit and reports he is looking very well. Apparently, he has taken to sleeping in front of the fridge, I don't know if that's because it is cooler and nearer the temperatures of the kennels which he is used to, or whether he just knows it contains food!

I've tried to make the most of the nice weather and treat today as a day off. It really has been so beautiful. I say this as I sit in the sunshine now, at five twenty three pm, with my T Shirt off and writing up the last three days.

So much has happened since the lockdown began, documenting it takes so much time. I know when this is over, the book you are reading will be something I will be very proud of, if nothing more than me completing a challenge of trying to document all which has gone on. It has been a daily commitment which has been difficult to address at times, but once it is completed it will hopefully mean one thing. We have gotten through this, we have survived.

Day Thirty Three.

Saturday 25th April 2020

UK Hospital Deaths: 813 taking the total to 20,319

Confirmed Cases: 148,377

- UK breaks through the 20,000 death mark, meaning we are one of only five nations to do so. The USA, Italy, Spain and France are the others.
- Key workers trying to book a test for coronavirus are in for a longer wait, as all the available slots were booked within an hour of the government reopening the website this morning.
- Britain's biggest steel producer, Tata Steel, has approached the government for support in the form of a funding package worth £500 million. Global orders have slumped due to coronavirus, as car manufacturers ceased production all across Europe.
- Two identical twins, Emma and Katy Davis (37) have both died of COVID-19 within three days of each other. The nurses both had the same underlying health condition.
- Thousands of patients are to be given iPads whilst in intensive care, in a new initiative called "iComms for ICU's." Already in excess of a thousand people have benefitted from over 200 devices and in some cases, the iPads have been used by dying patients to say goodbye to their loved ones.
- A trial involving drones delivering medical supplies to St Mary's Hospital on the Isle of Wight is to begin next week.

It was another night of broken sleep last night, as Haden had one of his clusters of fits. You may remember earlier in the book, I described how violent his seizures can be. Last night was no exception.

Haden arrived to us in the snowy winter of early 2013. Young, mischievous, you would never think he only had three legs.

His front left limb is missing, I don't know why and probably never will. On his arrival, I called every vets in the area to see if they had carried out what looks like very well performed surgery. Surely somebody somewhere knew where such a distinctive dog came from. Nothing.

I fell in love with his character immediately and started dropping hints to Rachel I was going to take him home, to which the reply came something like "you have enough." I knew though, he would win her over.

Next time she was in at the kennels I noticed she went straight to see him. I said nothing. Likewise, when I found them both cuddled in front of the heater in the office as the snow fell heavily outside.

After a discussion about whether he should come home or not, I still had enough dogs already apparently, Rachel put him back in his kennel and we both went out to walk more dogs.
On returning, I popped into the office to warm my hands, but couldn't get near the heater for a stretched out and very comfortable three legged, black Lurcher.

Rachel wasn't far behind me, and I jumped the gun a little and told her no matter how cute he was, he couldn't just be left in the office on his own. The look on her face told me she knew as little about him being there as I did. The two of us completely confused, we went to observe his kennel. What we saw was beyond belief.

Our new best friend had obviously loved the heat and comfort so much, he had taken it upon himself to chew the bars of his kennel front, flattening them just enough so he could squeeze his limbless front shoulder through, followed by the rest of his body. If I hadn't seen the sights of him in front of the heater and the state of the bars, I honestly wouldn't have believed it.

"Looks like he needs to come home then." Was all Rachel muttered almost under her breath.

We got snowed in at the kennels that day. Thankfully I had my Land Rover Defender with me, as there was no way Rachel's Astra was getting out of the farmyard. We set off on a dangerous but very pretty journey home into the Cheviots. Myself driving, Rachel in the passenger seat, and Haden as we had decided to call him, cosy in the middle.

At this point, we had no idea he was epileptic. Nothing showed for several weeks, then one by one I noticed him having seizures. Epilepsy is a condition I have no experience of. I know nobody who has it, only once had I seen a dog have a fit, until I lived with Haden.

The vets, we weren't using Emily for out of hours at the time, checked him over but wanted to restrain from putting him on medication until we could see just how bad his seizures were and see if there was a pattern.

Then a night that can only be described as horrific arrived. It was a Saturday. My daughter Neve was staying with me. She will have been about six at the time, I think. In the early hours Haden started fitting. Then there was another one, then there was another one, then another. I was on the phone to vets every twenty minutes or so asking for advice and help. In the end he was fitting about every five minutes. At 2am I scooped Neve up in her quilt and rushed him into the vets. Stotting around the back of the Defender this time, as the fits continued.

He stayed at the vets for a couple of days, on a massive dose of medication which meant he didn't even recognise me when I went in to visit him.

Incredibly his fighting spirit shone through again and eventually he was allowed home. He has been in medication ever since, and never has he been as been as vulnerable to a series of fits as he was that Saturday night.

I would say out of all the dogs I have had the pleasure of sharing my home with, Haden's illness makes him the most difficult. He is so amazingly brave and robust, but also so delicate and vulnerable.

Every time he has a fit, I think back to that day in the snow when we were completely unaware of his illness. I think then about the Saturday which ran into the early hours of Sunday morning and I know if he had still been in kennels, he would have died that night.

I think he knew he needed to get out of the kennel environment, his life depended on it, which is why he did what he did.

Swapping the fake heat of an old fashioned electric heater in the portacabin for the raw flames of a log fire at home, maybe he isn't so daft as he sometimes appears.

Day Thirty Four.

Sunday 26th April 2020

UK Hospital Deaths: 413 taking the total to 20,732

Confirmed Cases: 152,840

- Boris Johnson will finally return to work tomorrow and will immediately face pressure from Labour for not revealing an 'exit strategy' for lifting the UK's lockdown procedures. Whilst his stand in, Dominic Raab says it is not yet responsible to announce how lockdown measures could be relieved.
- Children in Spain have felt freedom for the first time in six weeks, after the Spanish Government began to ease lockdown restrictions.
- More than 100 mobile coronavirus testing units manned by 1,000 soldiers will hit the roads this week coming as the Government battle to reach its target of 100,000 tests a day.

The last thirty six hours has seen this crisis really hit home. I know everyone is in the same boat, we all have our lives on hold until this passes, but I can't help feeling the way I feel.

I miss my family and how life used to be. I miss the dogs and I miss having the help and support of the people who give up their time for free to ease the burden of the jobs of the day. I miss being with other people.

I don't know why the wall has suddenly hit me smack in the face, nor why it has chosen now to do it, but it certainly has hit me for six.

I have no motivation or strength. The will to succeed in all of this seems to have disappeared along with my freedom and the very weak form of social life I had before all of this broke out.

I am tired and frustrated, anxious and institutionalised within my weekly routine. I feel like giving in.

Tomorrow I am back with the dogs, still unable to do what I do best by working with them, but I need to motivate myself to make the most of the time I have with them. They need the support more than I do; we are all they have.

Day Thirty Five.

Monday 27th April 2020

UK Hospital Deaths: 360 taking the total to 21,092. The lowest increase since 30th March.

Confirmed Cases: 157,149

- Boris Johnson returns to work and addresses the nation from outside 10 Downing Street. He claims the UK is "turning the tide against the coronavirus" but then adds "this is not the time to relax the nationwide lockdown." He added "I ask you to contain your impatience, because I believe we are coming to the end of the first phase of this conflict and in spite of all the suffering we have so nearly succeeded."
- Health Secretary Matt Hancock announces the families of frontline NHS workers or social care staff who die from COVID-19 will each receive a £60,000 pay-out.
- GP's have been sent an urgent alert about the increasing number of children becoming seriously ill with coronavirus like symptoms.
- Dr Kari Stefansson says the coronavirus was already widespread in the UK at the very start of the pandemic and a lack of vigilance allowed the virus to spread to such catastrophic levels.
- The chancellor Rishi Sunak announces the Government will offer small businesses a coronavirus aid scheme of loans up to £50,000, which will be guaranteed by the Government.

Just when you don't want it to happen, life comes along and bites you. In my case today, it was literally!
Bobby is a little Shar Pei cross Staffordshire Bull Terrier, a quaint little character who came to us with a history of biting.

In his time here there have been several other incidents, usually involving food and his bed, but he is a dog which I have a good relationship with.

It took a long time to build that trust up, as he is so aloof and selective of who he interacts with, but I think it's fair to say I am the nearest anybody is to being 'his person.'

Whilst other people can walk him, there are others that he won't even allow into his kennel to feed him. Such is the complexity and stubbornness of his character. Some would say typical Shar Pei.

This morning I put him in one of the outside kennels as normal and gave him a roll type chew to occupy him whilst his kennel was cleaned. After placing the next dog in the kennel next to him, I saw blood on Bobby's kennel floor then saw him frantically rubbing his face on the tarmac. Such was the ferocity of his actions, he was making his chin and mouth bleed, he was also frothing from the mouth. I automatically began to worry, it looked as if he was choking.

I stopped for just a second to work out the pros and cons of going in to help, but if he was choking there was no choice. I entered his kennel.

At first, he seemed to understand what I was trying to do, he stopped scraping his face when I touched his head, he even allowed me to hold his bleeding chin and have a look inside his mouth.

It was then I saw he had bitten the chew into pieces and ate all of them but one, which was now wedged across the pallet at the top of his mouth. Still there was no negative reaction from him so, I made the decision to try and dislodge it.

Gently placing my fore finger on the chew, there was no reaction, but as soon as I tried to move the obstruction the whole situation changed in a split second.

When you are bitten by a dog, it all happens so quickly. You don't really have time to assess your reactions, your brain just quickly transforms from shock mode to survival. You aren't really aware of what is happening or what you are doing, it just all happens too fast to compute at the time.

As I pushed against the chew, Bobby growled and attacked. Quite clearly it must have been painful for him, he reacted in the only way perhaps a dog can when pain is inflicted on him.

The first bite came instantly, then the second, then the third. I remember trying to talk to him, telling him it was me, calling his name so he would realise.

Fourth bite, fifth bite, sixth bite. I think in all he must have come at me eight or nine times before I was actually able to get a firm enough grip on his neck to restrict him from leaping at me and grabbing hold of whatever he could with his teeth. With me back in control I was able to hold him down until I manoeuvred myself out of his kennel.

It is then the reality began to surface. I looked down at my right hand and wrist, lacerated by teeth. My left forearm was also dripping blood and had several lines of teeth shaped crevasses along it. Bobby went back to smashing his face off the ground. It wasn't until later on, I wondered if the fact an alien object had been bracing the top of his mouth, had saved the bites from being deeper and more severe.

I walked into the kennels, a journey which now I can't remember making, my chest was sore and there was blood seeping through my t shirt from my stomach. Collette saw me first, the shock written all over her face when she saw the blood dripping from my hand. I shouted for Rachel to come, then I retrieved the pole or 'rigid lead' as I call it, and a metal temporary fence post which has a hook shape on one end. It's the kind of post you see at events when barriers made from tape are put up to keep people out of areas. The one I have at the kennels has gotten us out of some very difficult situations in the past. Today was no exception.

Returning to the back run, I put my hand around the kennel door and got Bobby on the rigid lead after a bit of a struggle. Once out I handed it to Rachel as I thought it would be safer for her to be at that end of the equipment.

Thrashing himself around, now because of the discomfort in his mouth and being held, Bobby wasn't making this easy. Every time I got the fence post near his mouth he would react; Rachel couldn't hold him. We swapped apparatus and I took a firmer hold of him. Pushing him up against the tough compound wall made of old railway sleepers, I was careful I didn't hurt him, but I also had to be firm. The only way Rachel would be able to release the chew would be if I could keep him still enough so she could make good contact.

After four or five attempts she managed to free it. Bobby's reaction? He chewed it like he had the rest of it! I put him back in his outside kennel as Collette had come to help and his main place of residence still needed cleaned. She went off to do that, whilst Rachel took me into the office to address the extent of my injuries.

Taking my t shirt off, there was severe swelling and bruising to my right breast already, two marks where canines had punctured the skin where the only parts still flesh coloured. Purples, blacks and reds were already beginning to take over, like an oil leak in a puddle. Within the hour I had a huge lump, swelling the like of which I have never seen before.

My stomach was also changing colour quickly, again teeth marks and small puncture wounds had invaded that part of my body and had begun to take over. This was going to hurt.

Once cleaned up and bandaged, I had to face up to the task of getting Bobby back inside his kennel. He is one of the handful of dogs of which I am the only one on my team which handles them. Whilst I was a little nervous, the reasons behind the incident were already clear in my head. I understood why there had been such a reaction from him, I know that pain was the reason he lashed out. This wasn't just an attack for 'no reason.'

I opened the kennel door cautiously, his tail was wagging, pleased to see me like normal. I put his lead on, gave him a couple of strokes on the head, then walked him back. Not once did I feel he was going to turn on me again, whilst being very careful and alert, I was also relieved the incident hadn't seemed to affect our relationship. In the afternoon we went for a nice walk as normal.

The knock on effect from all of this was we were now way behind in what is already a strenuous schedule. Jax had been collecting food and bedding donations from the drop of points around Alnwick, when she came to drop it all off and saw what had happened, she offered to help. I agreed.

I had been mulling over an idea in my mind the last few days about how we could look to lighten the pressure which was on each member of both teams, but the priority had to be to keep everybody safe and protected.

Jon had released an 'emergency plan' to all the staff and volunteers stating our policies if either myself or Rich caught the virus. There was also a plan documented for if a member of staff went down ill too. Both really consisted of having a single volunteer per team on standby, the only real condition was they had to be available for the three shifts their particular team did. Although we knew it was a huge request, all volunteers were asked if they were either interested or available to do such shifts. Obviously, some have work commitments, some have family commitments, but two people said they were available and wanted to help. Jax and Naomi.

I rang Jon to discuss the idea of making a slight moderation to the way we operate and to make the teams up from three to four with immediate effect. He agreed as long as the members of both teams were happy with the introduction of a fourth member, then we should go ahead.

After discussions, it was agreed. Jax became a member of my team with Naomi joining Rich's. Whilst I understand it is a bit like placing all of our eggs in one basket (or should that be two baskets) it means hopefully the pressure will reduce, some of the other duties such as tidying and sorting may now also be achievable, whilst more importantly, the dogs should have a little bit more attention.

Day Thirty Six.

Tuesday 28th April 2020

UK Hospital Deaths: 586 taking the total to 21,678. Matt Hancock announces from tomorrow the government's daily figures will include both those in care homes and the community.

Confirmed Cases: 161,145

- Boris Johnson leads the nation in a minute's silence for all the key worker who have lost their lives in the battle against this hideous disease.
- The Health Secretary insists protecting care home patients from COVID-19 is "a top priority" emphasising the huge failings of the Conservative Government to protect the elderly and most vulnerable. It is reported there were 4,343 coronavirus deaths reported by care home providers in England in the last two weeks.
- The Government also expands its policy on testing for coronavirus, as it announces over 65's and the people who need to leave their homes for work are now eligible. They also state those living in the same households as the aforementioned will be eligible for testing if they show symptoms.
- British Airways is set to make 12,000 staff redundant following the collapse in the travel market. The figure is more than a quarter of the company's workforce.
- The number of people confirmed as positive for coronavirus in the USA breaks the one million mark, as cases double in the last 18 days. At least 1,002,498 positive infections have been confirmed. Spain are second with at least 232,000. More than 56,400 Americans have died with the virus, an average of about 2,000 per day this month.

- Royal Mail announces the alarming news they are temporarily scrap delivering mail on a Saturday, to ease the 'burden' on its workers. Surely, they should be improving their service in such a time of international crisis when people are housebound and dependent on parcel deliveries to survive as well as letters and cards being vital in being able to connect with loved ones who they cannot see because of lockdown.
- Estate agent website Zoopla claim around 373,000 property transactions worth a total of £82bn are on hold because of the complications of the coronavirus.

Having made the decision yesterday, today was the first day we operated as a four. The difference it made was immediate. The way we have been operating has been with two people cleaning the kennels and one taking the dogs in and out of the outside kennels. It is obvious just how much of a hard job the kennel cleaning is, but the other role is equally hard work.

On my team it is usually me which does the majority of the swaps, which in itself is very trashing. The whole system only works if everybody works together and you get into a routine, so the timing is right. Bringing the correct dog once their kennel is clean, whilst then replacing it with another. Keeping the more reactive dogs separate from others by leaving an empty kennel in-between, and of course the outside kennels need cleaned between dogs too.

Operating with two cleaning and two swapping suddenly alleviated the intensity, you had two pairs each working with their partner but also as a group on the whole. We got finished cleaning the kennels an hour and a half quicker than we had been of late.

The extra time allowed us to do other duties. The food store got a little bit of a sort out, the back run got a good hose down, the kitchen area tidied. I put my time to use to sort through bags of things which had been donated and sat on my desk for weeks.

All very useful, there were things in those bags which I didn't realise we had. Medication, specialised shampoos and leads all things which will get used and for which we are extremely grateful.

There was one thing though which stood out which we could use straight away, a magnetic collar. I have used these in the past for treating dogs with arthritis. Haden has one he has worn for years to help with his epilepsy. I am no expert at how they work or why, but I think they do help, very much in the same way people with arthritis wear magnetic bracelets. With Merlin still limping, as we wait to be able to get him in for x-rays, I thought it might help him.

He has looked a little bit down of late and also been sick a few times. I have to admit I am worried about him. Rottweilers are prone to osteosarcoma's (bone tumours) and we have had several through the rescue who have suffered from them. Whilst there is no obvious lump or bumps I can see, it's a bit concerning going onto pain relief such as Metacam does not seemed to have helped.

Today I have changed his food to a sensitive stomach variety, he is now wearing his nice new red magnetic collar and all the staff have been made aware of how I feel. We will all be paying close attention to him and keeping a record to see if any of the changes we make help.

Day Thirty Seven.

Wednesday 29th April 2020

UK Deaths: For the first time this includes the figures of people losing their lives from COVID-19 in care homes and the community. The days hospital death total was 765 with a backdated amount of 3,811 from other areas, taking the overall total to 26,097.

Confirmed Cases: 165,221

- The UK now has the second highest death toll in Europe (behind Italy with 26,872) and the third highest in the world after Italy and the USA who has recorded over 59,000.
- Michael Gove, the Chancellor of the Duchy of Lancaster, has said the UK's islands maybe the first areas to lift lockdown measures in a pilot scheme for easing restrictions.
- Gavin Williamson, the Education Secretary, has said school children will not all return to school at the same time, and he expects them to still be at home until the autumn at least. Using countries such as Germany and Denmark as an example.
- Children under the age of 10 have been told they are now allowed to hug their grandparents in Switzerland, as the country begins to reduce their lockdown measures.

It was another busy but fulfilling day today, as again the extended team seemed to make a difference. More tidying, more sorting in the extra time created by taking less time to clean, the day almost felt like how it used to be.

With Jax now fully committed to a more hands on role, her husband Darron has very kindly offered to continue the job of collecting the donations on his own. Today he did the rounds and collected another unbelievable haul.

People have been so supportive and so kind throughout this crisis, I'd actually say we have more of everything than we have ever had before. It feels as if the public have realised just how special our dogs are and have really gone out of their way to help us give them everything.

Two days after the incident with Bobby, I am pleased to say our relationship doesn't seem to have suffered. If anything, I would say it has strengthened it from my side. I now have first-hand experience of just what he is capable of and know he will react if pushed. I wish I hadn't of course, but I have an understanding of what he has been through before now which in turn brings an even greater form of respect.

At some point in his life somebody has hurt him. Which explains the trust issue and why he is difficult to get to know. However, the incident on Monday shows the severity of the hurt he has suffered. He did not take a second to think about what he was about to do, his instant reaction and only response was to attack and defend himself.

My wounds are healing, but sore. The deepest ones are between my thumb and fore finger on my right hand, very inconsiderate considering I am completely right handed. I think perhaps the sorest ones though are those on my stomach. There must be some muscle damage as every time a dog pulls me there is a sharp dagger like pain. They will heal though, I have been through this so many times before, it is just a shame the pain Bobby has suffered previously may never have the same healing qualities.

Day Thirty Eight.

Thursday 30th April 2020

Total UK Deaths: 674 taking the total to 26,771

Confirmed Cases: 171,253

AM

- Justice secretary Robert Buckland has admitted it is probable the Government will miss its target of 100,000 coronavirus tests per day by the end of April, which of course is today. He did however, state the milestone would be hit within the next couple of days. Latest figures show capacity to test has reached 73,400 with 52,429 of those tests being used on Tuesday.
- There are only 33 countries and territories across the world which have not registered a case of the coronavirus. The majority of them are small, difficult to reach islands in the pacific, such as the Solomon Islands. There have now been over three million cases of the virus in 214 countries and territories recognised by the United Nations. There have been deaths in at least 166 of them.

PM

- Boris Johnson, on his first appearance for five weeks, has declared the UK is "past the peak and on the downward slope" of the corona virus outbreak, in the Governments daily address to the nation. He then went on to say, "at no stage has our NHS been overwhelmed, no patient went without a ventilator, no patient was deprived of intensive care."
- He also revealed the figure for testing the public for the virus reached 81,611 tests on Wednesday. Nearly twenty

- thousand short of the target of 100,000 by the end of today.
- Mr Johnson also promised he would reveal a "comprehensive plan" next week on how he intends to restart the economy and lifting some lockdown measures.
- B&Q have fully reopened all of their 288 stores, despite the UK still being in a state of lockdown.

So, according to Boris Johnson we are now past the peak and only have to wait another week until things can begin to get back to normal. I'm not sure in reality it will be so simple.

Sitting in the comfort of Chequers, whilst the normal people who make this country tick over are stuck in their own homes and unable to work to provide for their family, I'm sure paints a rosier picture than the one we are all facing.

Today is the first day of my self-imposed three day isolation. Three days of going nowhere but within my own domain to protect myself from others who haven't been as resilient.

Only tomorrow is my daughter's fourteenth birthday. I really want to see her, having not done so for almost six weeks. Tomorrow I will have to brave the outside world and see just exactly what is going on. It feels like travelling into the big city for the first time as a kid. The safety and tranquillity of where I live, means I really do not know what it will be like in Bedlington. I am filled with dread but also a little tinge of excitement. It is a crazy time.

After falling victim of the downward spiral of depression on my last three days away from the kennels, I am also concerned it will happen again this time. Last time I felt as if my whole life was in limbo, totally out of range of any influence by me. The cabin fever had begun to kick in and I'd lost any motivation to continue on.

This time I am determined the same won't happen. I intend to use the time wisely and put the pressures, conflicts and stresses of my other life to one side for now.

Today I have caught up with admin things, gift aid again, paid the staff's national insurance etc, etc. Tonight, I have started to decorate the downstairs bathroom, a job I have never really had any interest in or desire for. It needs doing though, so it will be done.

     Boris says we are on the way out of this, I'm not sure I agree, but if that is the case, having three days off in a row may become a luxury I don't get very often. If it does turn out that way, I intend to make the most of them whilst I have them.

Day Thirty Nine.

Friday 1st May 2020

Total UK Deaths: 739 taking the total now to 27,510

Confirmed Cases: 177,454

- A spokesperson for Boris Johnson claims there is evidence wearing face masks have a "weak but positive" effect in reducing the transmission of COVID-19.
- David Icke's Facebook page is taken down by the social media website, after the conspiracy theorist spread unsubstantiated stories about COVID-19 being connected to 5G.
- Sisters Danielle Pryor (34) and Sarah Pryor (33) are jailed for 26 and 14 weeks respectively for attacking, spitting and coughing at police officers after being confronted about breaking lockdown rules.
- The Premier League continues to push ahead with plans to complete the 2019-2020 season in June, despite health concerns being raised from the league's players. The plan includes that all matches would be held within a group of ten neutral stadiums and behind closed doors and testing all players and staff for the virus twice a week.
- Body cam footage emerges of Temisan Oritsejafor spitting blood in the eyes of PC Annie Napier, whilst being placed under arrest for assault. Mr Oritsejafor was already on bail for attacking another police officer a few weeks ago.

The first of May 2006 was the day my daughter Neve was born, today is her fourteenth birthday and I have to face up to the fact I won't be able to give her a hug or a birthday kiss.

    It is six weeks since I saw her last. Once lockdown came into force, I took the decision to minimise the risk of infection for both of us, as at the time nobody knew how long this was going to last or how serious it would become. I miss her dearly, but I know she is afraid of going outside and the risk of catching coronavirus. It must be so difficult to understand at her age, how the world she has known all her life has suddenly stopped. Everything she has known has changed so much.

After discussions with her mam I have decided to go and see her for a little while, whilst keeping stringently to the social distancing rules. Over the last few weeks, I have bought her gifts, every single one coming via the dependable and fantastic Amazon delivery drivers, I want to get those to her and watch her open them. Seeing their children open presents on their birthday or at Christmas is something every parent savours. For those few minutes it might even seem as if things are ok, normality restored in these mad times.

It is also nearly six weeks since I broke out of the protective bubble of my home, work and the little Co-op in Rothbury. I have been to no towns or large supermarkets, I have no concept of the reality, which is going on in the big, outside world.

As I leave home, I feel a little nervous and apprehensive. I check on numerous occasions I have a bottle of hand sanitiser in my pocket, it also feels extremely strange putting on clothes other than my works gear or a pair of shorts and a hoodie. Something so simple and habitual now feels like an expedition into the unknown, a mission to Mars. I don't like the feeling.

En route I have to say I am a little in shock at how busy the A1 is. Not as jammed as it would be on a normal Friday, more like a Sunday, but still the streams of cars on the road is a contrast to seeing only vans and lorries like I have done every other day whilst travelling to work.

Every car I pass, or passes me, I look through the window at the driver and passengers, wondering where they are going. Do they really need to be out? Is their journey so vital they risk the obvious dangers of infection? Or maybe it has been like this all along, only I haven't seen it in my goldfish bowl of a world for the last six weeks.

I reach the Stannington turn off and venture through Netherton, the roads are just as busy, but the paths are quiet. The windows of the big houses are all decorated with handmade rainbow pictures, like Rachel told me the ones in Morpeth are, all thanking the NHS. I pass one which simply says, "Thank you Key Workers."

Once I arrive at the outskirts of Bedlington, it is a slightly different story. People are everywhere, walking their dogs, carrying bags of shopping. It is surreal knowing I have locked myself away for so long, whilst others have been out and about, carrying on with life regardless.

Every supermarket I pass there is a queue outside. People standing two metres apart, clutching a colourful collection of bags for life. The shoppers are of all ages, I have been so lucky in being able to get the food and essentials I need in the ways I have. I don't think I would have the patience to live like this.

I pull up outside Neve's house and her mam opens the door, asking me not to touch any of the handles. She isn't being awkward or offensive, just safe, I agree with her caution, but it feels very strange.

I wish Neve Happy Birthday and give her the gifts I have brought, carefully sanitising my hands again before I do so. She seems pleased to see me, but admits she feels a little awkward having not seen me for so long. Then she asks me to stand at the opposite side of the room as she opens her presents.

I am not offended once more, but it is a difficult thing to accept I can't sit on the sofa next to her whilst she does. She is fourteen and knows enough about what is happening in the news to keep herself safe, I do as she asks.

Neve facetimes her Nan and Mike whilst I am there to say thank you for her gifts they ordered online and got delivered straight there. I haven't seen my mam or Mike for as long as I haven't seen Neve. The regular Wednesday catch up and pizza with the four of us seems so long ago now. So much has changed and I miss those times.

Then I leave. No hugs, no goodbye kisses. I tell Neve to enjoy the rest of the day then make my way to the door which Elaine has already opened.

Outside people are still everywhere, I feel a knot begin to develop in the pit of my stomach, as the urge to get back to the safety of my own little world intensifies.

I've been outside for just over two hours and feel relief as I pull up outside my front door. It has been amazing seeing my daughter and I am pleased I made the effort to do so. She is growing up so fast and I am very proud of her.

The journey made me realise though, just how strange a time this all is. Seeing people queueing up for food as if we were living through some kind of major war, the ignorance of some who are still defying the lockdown regulations, the hustle and bustle of people trying to carry on with their lives with as much normality as possible. They all make me feel both safe and vulnerable at the same time. I maybe alone here, which is hard at times, but I don't have the pressure of protecting myself from others. Living in constant fear must be all consuming.

Just as I was about to leave to go to Neve's I had a phone call from Jon. Catherine (Team B) has been sent home by Rich for feeling unwell. Sensible management, but also a worry. Rich has asked her to stay off tomorrow too, which will give her four days to recover. The obvious worry of the virus is the 'unsaid' subject matter of our conversation.

Day Forty.

Saturday 2nd May 2020

Total UK Deaths: 621 taking the total now to 28,131

Confirmed Cases: 182,260

- Government passes its target of carrying out 100,000 coronavirus tests per day before the end of April, as Matt Hancock announces 122,347 people were tested for COVID-19 in the 24 hours leading up to 9am yesterday morning. However, there is some controversy attached to that figure. Up until now the daily figures only included tests which had been sent to laboratories. This total, however, now includes tests which have been sent out to homes and the testing sites. In the last 24 hours 27,497 home kits were delivered, whilst 12,872 tests were carried out in mobile locations. All of which means if the Government had continued to measure the number of tests as it had done previously, the figure would have only been 81,978, resulting in another failure by Boris Johnson and his Government.
- Queues have built up outside council rubbish tips, as they open their doors for the first time since lockdown commenced, putting more pressure on the Government to start lifting restrictions.
- Ireland is extending its lockdown policy but is lifting some restrictions to allow people to travel further for exercise and allowing the over 70's leave their homes for a walk or a drive. These measures are all part of a five phase plan which will ease restrictions, each phase being three weeks apart. The plan aims to start on the 18th of May and should see the fifth phase commence on the 10th August if everything goes as planned. Movement to the next phase will only be introduced if the virus remains

- under control. If death figures or confirmed cases begin to rise again, the country will move back a phase.
- A trial has begun to see if plasma rich in antibodies from the blood of people who have beaten COVID-19, could help others fight the virus. Blood is taken from a volunteer's arm, the plasma removed, then returned to the host. If successful, it would mean patients who are critically unwell from coronavirus could receive a transfusion of the plasma to help fight the disease.

I received a text message from Catherine this morning to say she feels a little better and is putting it down to some kind of stomach bug. She sounds as relieved as I am.

Part of the conversation with Jon yesterday was about drafting in a replacement for Catherine as she manages quite a few of the more difficult dogs.

I authorised Rich to contact Michael who seems an obvious choice as he manages very similar dogs, in true team spirit, Michael steps up.

It must be so hard from a volunteer's point of view, not being able to stick to the routine you have done for years by coming to the kennels. It must also be so difficult to cope with missing the wonderful characters we have all grown to love. I spoke to Michael last night; he couldn't wait to get up there this morning.

I have been asked to help a dog which is at the vets today to be destroyed. A two and a half year old Rottweiler, his crime was growling at a young niece as she tried to take a chew from his mouth. Throw in the fact he had been fighting with the family's other dog, the owners felt it was reason enough to end his life.

It was a nurse from a vet's we normally help, but the madness of this worldwide pandemic means I had to say no. We are struggling to cope with what we have; another difficult dog would tip the whole operation over the edge. There is also the complication of getting it to us. It's a sickening feeling to have to be responsible for whether a dog lives or dies, but what else can I do?

I mention a couple of other rescues who I believe may still be taking in dogs, in the hope there may be one in a more fortunate position than us. A little while later I hear he has a space at one of the places I mentioned. Fantastic news but also one which reopens the wounds of how I feel so useless in all of this.

I set this charity up to help the type of dog in this case, in the exact situation he found himself. He is now the latest in a growing list of dogs I have had to say no to because of the situation and the pressure we are under. It was happening way before lockdown, but the monotony of our everyday lives at present just amplifies the fact we can no longer do what I set us out to do. It feels like we have become a victim of our own success and because of that we are pushed beyond our very limit. I know people will reply to this by saying you can't save them all, which is very true, but it really hurts. The dogs always stay in my mind until I know they are safe. I know I can't be held responsible, but once I have been involved it eats away at me. As I said in the BBC documentary Inside Out a couple of years ago, the minute I stop trying to save them all, is the minute I need to stop.

Day Forty One.

Sunday 3rd May 2020

Total UK Deaths: 315 taking the total to 28,446

Confirmed Cases: 186,599

- Cabinet minister Michael Gove admits the Government has made mistakes during this crisis and also reveals only 76,496 tests were carried out in the last 24 hours. Well below the target of 100,000 and once again raises questions how the figures which enabled the Government to meet its own target were reached.
- Former Tory pensions minister Baroness Altmann claims older people will "rebel and risk prison" if they are forced to continue to isolate whilst other lockdown restrictions are eased. She claims it would be "age discrimination" and would lead to social unrest.
- The Isle of Wight will trial an NHS contact tracing app this week. Transport Secretary Grant Shapps explained how the app would "alert people if they've been near somebody who is later diagnosed with having coronavirus."
- Boris Johnson reveals he became so ill whilst in intensive care with coronavirus, a strategy was drawn up in case he died. "There was a stage when I was thinking, 'How am I going to get out of this?"
- Germany announce plans for sending some children back to school in a small but significant move towards normality.
- At least 10 mosques in the UK have created temporary mortuaries to help cope with the huge amount of Muslim deaths in areas such as Birmingham and London. Prayer Halls have been filled with coffins in preparation, whilst

- some mosques have 40ft refrigerated containers in their car parks which can store up to thirty bodies.
- Brighton and Hove Albion are the first Premier League club to publicly oppose the plan to see out the remainder of the season in neutral stadiums. Chief executive Paul Barber says at "this critical point in the season it would have a material effect on the integrity of the competition."
- Rolls Royce is reportedly planning to axe up to 8,000 jobs as aircraft manufacturers cut production dramatically due to the coronavirus pandemic.

It's always a strange feeling going back to the kennels, I know it's an issue that I need to work on, but I always have it in the back of my mind when I'm not there.

I have to say though the introduction of a 'close down list' at the end of my last shift seems to have made a huge difference. Going in this morning the place was in great shape and it meant we were able to get straight onto looking after the dogs.

I think everyone has been working so hard to give all we can to the dogs, some of the basics have been forgotten. Not deliberately, just overlooked. That includes us all.

The introduction of the list means once everything is signed off, the place is ready for the next shift, saving valuable time.

Team B have clearly worked so hard yesterday, getting all the little jobs done, but also getting twenty of the forty nine dogs which we currently have in the kennels, out for a third walk. An amazing achievement and one which hands the gauntlet over to us on our three days in.

I spoke to Michael on the night-time, he had a great day and loved seeing all the dogs again. I fully appreciate him going in to help, and despite the fact he was exhausted afterwards, I know how worthwhile he felt it had been.

One thing I did notice today was our levels of bedding are beginning to drop, as dogs rip blankets or even worse make a mess on them. I feel we have asked the outside world for so much, which is still producing daily deliveries, so on this one we should try to appeal a little nearer to home at first.

I have asked all the staff and Jax and Naomi, who are also on each of our three shifts, to ask family, friends and neighbours if they have any old bedding, towels etc which could be left at peoples doors and then brought up on that staff members shifts. Hopefully, it will produce some positive results, it will also limit the need of collections that a public appeal would have created.

Day Forty Two.

Monday 4th May 2020

Total UK Deaths: 288 bringing the total to 28,734 (the lowest daily increase since the end of March.

Confirmed Cases:

- Big news is expected from Boris Johnson on Sunday, as it is expected that he will reveal the UK's full lockdown exit strategy. Although lockdown restrictions were due to expire on Thursday, the country is still being kept in the dark.
- The Government also announce there were 85,186 tests carried out in the last twenty four hours. Once again falling short of their target of 100,000.
- Public urged to download the NHS contact tracing app, believing it may be an important part of beating the virus.
- Figures released by the Government show more than one in five British workers have now been furloughed, meaning the state is paying the wages of 6.3 million people. 800,000 employers have made claims of 80% of their staff's wages, at a cost of £8bn so far.
- New Zealand report no new cases of COVID-19 on Monday, indicating that the country's firm approach to eliminate the virus has worked.
- Old test results confirm the coronavirus was present in France as long ago as December. Checking back over the history of patients hospitalised with respiratory issues has confirmed COVID-19 was active then.
- The purpose built NHS Nightingale Hospital in London is to revert to stand by, as the level of coronavirus infections in London drop.

- US Secretary of state Mike Pompeo says there is a "significant amount of evidence" the current COVID-19 outbreak originated from a laboratory in Wuhan, China.

I keep using the word recovery, but it's just something which is constantly running through my head. I think people think once lockdown is reduced the world will just bounce back to normal and everything will be ok. I think some people may even have forgotten the troubles they had in their lives before everything was confined to such a tiny existence.

For me, the hard work will start once this is over. The amazing response to our appeal has secured our survival for a little while, hopefully long enough to get us through the restricted period. But what happens after that? It's certainly not going to be a case of opening the shop's front door and a stream of people will be standing there with buckets of money to spend. People are still going to be frightened to go outside and be around strangers, some people will not have jobs to go back to and will therefore have no money, businesses will have to try and attract customers all over again.

It will be like starting all over again, only with the bittersweet feeling of knowing you can do it, you can make a success of things, you just have to do the hard work all over again.

For us as a charity, I think it provides us with a great opportunity to start over. We have had to make changes to our daily routines which, thanks to a lot of hard work and commitment, have worked. I will be implementing these changes into the way we run once volunteers are able to come back on site. This in turn though creates an opportunity to alter and tweak other procedures, which will then benefit the dogs even more.

Some days in the past we have been left short-handed, others there have been too many people and the day turns into a bit of a free for all. Coming out of this seems a perfect opportunity to try and make sure neither happen again.

Today I sent the following message to all the volunteers. I think it was a positive thing to do for several reasons, but also it reminds them they haven't been forgotten and they still have a huge part to play in driving the charity forward.

I also understand that some people's circumstances may have changed, and they may not be able or want to commit their time to us anymore. By sending this, it gives people an easy method of walking away.

For me personally though, it means once I know what everyone's intentions are, I can start looking at some of the ideas which are running through my head. Over the next few days, I can come up with a blueprint of how we will operate once we are in 'recovery.'

"Good morning, I hope you're all keeping well and safe. Just a quick update to let you know that we're all doing ok and today should be the 75th day in a row that everyone has been out at least twice.

Moving forward, we think one of the reasons that we have been so successful in keeping things running is that we have always tried to stay one step ahead.

With this in mind we are beginning to look at the charity's recovery plans and how we can hit the ground running once lockdown restrictions are lifted.

There will be changes to the daily routine that you remember, but all positive. For example, the way we have been cleaning has worked incredibly well and will staying as part of our long-term initiative.

We have to say it maybe weeks or even months before there are any changes in how we operate, depending on the government's guidelines. That is all out of our control, but we aim to have things in place once we are able to open our doors to you all again.

Your contribution of time and effort will still be a vital part of the day to day running and will be structured so they help the dogs in the most beneficial way.

We are still looking at how that would work, but in the meantime we need to gather stock of who wants to still be involved and what time they have available.

If you all could please message me (Stephen) privately (not on this group chat) stating whether you still want to be involved and a rough indication of time you're looking to give (it is ESSENTIAL that you add this) then we can start planning.

If I do not hear from you within 48 hours, I will take it that you no longer wish to volunteer, and your details will be removed from the volunteers register with no hard feelings.

In the mean-time thank you and stay safe."

What seems like forever ago, I ran a little competition on Facebook offering a free, signed copy of my book It's A Dog's Life. It was just to create a little interest and also to remind people of why I started this charity.
      The only condition I set was the winner must send me a review of the book, good or bad, I was willing to accept both. Recently the winner, a lady called Charlotte, sent me her review:

It's a Dog's Life

Being an animal lover & having two rescue dogs of my own I knew this was going to be an emotional read, with which I might struggle. When on the second or third page I already had tears in my eyes (I'm a big softie), I did contemplate not putting myself through it. However, I felt I owed it to dogs everywhere, toughened myself up and finished the book in one sitting.

The book is beautifully written, the story told through the eyes of a dog in the pound. Although a work of fiction, with a lot of truths encompassed, the author brilliantly portrays how life may feel & pan out for a dog that finds itself in such a situation. A situation which is all too common & an unfortunate harsh reality in this sometimes cruel world. The author educates the reader, cleverly incorporating many truths into the story by introducing characters with back stories that detail why many dogs find themselves abandoned & unloved by those they trusted unconditionally.

This book is a must read for any animal lover and in an ideal world would be an essential read for anybody thinking of owning a dog. It was, in one word, unputdownable, despite the occasional escaped tear and a good sob at the end. A highly recommended read, but definitely have the tissues to hand!

My writing is something that is very personal, and I hope it has improved since I wrote that book back in 2013. However, such a fantastic review means so much to me and gives me encouragement to continue. Thank you, Charlotte.

I posted the review on our website and within minutes copies were sold and money was raised. It all made me very proud.

I am also very proud of my team today, we looked at how we did things yesterday and dabbled with a few new practices. It all paid off today as we also managed to get twenty dogs out on three walks.

Day Forty Three.

Tuesday 5th May 2020

Total UK Deaths: 693 taking the total now to 29,427

Confirmed Cases: 194,990

- The UK now has the highest death toll in Europe, passing Italy with more COVID-19 related deaths. Today's total of 29,427 surpasses Italy's of 29,315.
- Data provided by Labour MP Stephen Doughty claims out of the 18.1 million people who arrived in the UK from all over the world, only 273 from China and Japan were taken to government isolation centres.
- Virgin Atlantic plans to axe up to a third of its workforce, with over 3,000 jobs expected to be cut.
- On the 3rd March, the SPI-B group of behavioural scientists were calling for the practice of shaking hands to be stopped. They warned the government directly. On the same day Boris Johnson told a Downing Street news conference he was continuing to shake hands of people he met.
- Scotland's First Minister Nicola Sturgeon reveals some options being considered to reduce lockdown restrictions. They include people being able to meet friends in small groups, but only outside. Other options being considered include some children being allowed back to school, relaxing the rules on daily exercise and clearing the way for business to reopen. However, she also said lifting any restrictions would be a gradual process and not like "flipping a switch."
- In Germany, Markus Soeder, governor of the south eastern state of Bavaria, announces beer gardens will reopen on the 18th May. Restaurants will open a week later but will be restricted to a limited number of

customers and limited opening hours, along with strict hygiene rules. Hotels will reopen on the 30th May, but their swimming pools and saunas will remain closed. More immediately, families will be able to visit elderly relatives from tomorrow. Bavaria (which includes Munich) had the highest per capita coronavirus infection rate in the whole of Germany.

The response to my message to the volunteers has been very positive. The consensus seems to be they all can't wait to get back, and the availability seems the same as before the public were incarcerated.

There has only been one person saying they no longer wish to volunteer, due to health reasons, whilst I am still waiting to hear back from one other. Not a bad result from twenty eight volunteers.

It now gives me a solid foundation to start looking at things and making plans. I suspect the lockdown measures will be reduced gradually rather than just opening the flood gates, so I too will probably have to stage the return. I do have some ideas in mind, such as volunteers taking dogs off site for walks rather than being in the kennels, once travelling restrictions loosen. This would then account for the persons exercise, and also keep us within the government's social distancing guidelines.

Obviously, it would need to be dogs who were used to their handlers and also comfortable with the outside world and getting in and out of cars, but it its feasible. Before lockdown, Jax and her husband Darron were taking dogs to the beach on a weekly basis. I guess my idea would be a similar thing.

It is all dependent of course on what changes are brought in by the Government and when. The present lockdown situation expires in two days on the 7th May. I would expect an extension but at the moment nobody knows.

It is widely being reported by the media on Sunday, Boris Johnson will announce his exit strategy, then everything will suddenly become clearer. Time will tell.

Day Forty Four.

Wednesday 6th May 2020

Total UK Deaths: 649 Taking the total now to 30,076

Confirmed Cases: 201,101

- The Prime Minister sets a new target of 200,000 tests per day by the end of May and says he "bitterly" regrets the crisis which has swept through the UK's care homes.
- Boris Johnson also says the UK could "get going" with easing some lockdown measures from Monday. This is despite the fact the UK has only just eclipsed Italy with the highest fatality rate in Europe.
- Perhaps even more alarming is the fact the Government have now missed their coronavirus testing target of 100,000 per day, for the fourth day in a row. The latest figures released show only 69,463 COVID-19 tests were conducted in the twenty four hours leading up to 9am today, which is a decline in totals of nearly 15,000.
- Debenhams have failed to reach an agreement with landlords over rent for its five stores in Reading, Croydon, Birmingham, Leicester and Glasgow Silverburn, meaning that all of those stores will not reopen after lockdown and 1,000 people will lose their jobs.
- Following on from the announcements from the Bavaria region of Germany, Chancellor Angela Merkel announces plans to ease the country's coronavirus restrictions. Household meet ups, reopening of shops and the resuming of the Bundesliga football season will all soon be permitted as part of phase two of the country dealing with the virus.

- Uber are another company which have announced job cuts because of the coronavirus pandemic, with 3,700 people to face unemployment.
- The 1.5 million people who are being "shielded" from coronavirus may be house bound for longer than the original twelve week period according to Health Secretary Matt Hancock.
- Ironically schools have begun to open in the Chinese city of Wuhan, where it is believed COVID-19 originated. Around 57,000 high school students wore face masks and walked in single file past thermal scanners, as they entered the buildings for the first time since the schools were closed down in January.

For the first time since the country was shut down and thrown into this uncertainty, I have treated today like a proper day off.

Ok, so I have updated the last couple of days in this book, but that is going to be a daily occurrence until all of this is over and whilst I wouldn't say I enjoy it, I feel that documenting history as it happens is something which is very important.

I have also looked into the Governments 'Coronavirus Self-Employment Income Support Scheme' of which I am eligible through running my own business called The Rescue Place. As a Trustee SHAK, I cannot be employed by them, but through my experience of handling such difficult dogs, I can offer a professional service.

It appears I am eligible for a grant but need to apply on May 15th. This is because a big part of what I do involves the out of hours stray collection for Northumberland Council. The night on which Boris Johnson announced he was putting the country into lockdown, I withdrew our services, resulting in a large monthly income deficit.

Apart from all of that, I have done nothing else. I woke up with the sun bleaching through my bedroom window, even now at 9pm it is still shining. The weather has been perfect, no wind and no cloud, I have done a lot of gardening and finished decorating the downstairs toilet. Simple jobs to most, but ones I simply do not have the time for in 'real life.'

Everywhere I look in the news it seems to say, 'lifting restrictions' or 'coming out of lockdown.' The weather today felt like summer had finally arrived and all the darkness and storms had finally passed, only this time for good.

I don't believe we are anywhere near out of this mess yet. I don't think the restrictions should be lifted when there are still so many people losing their lives. I worry about the chance of a second wave of this virus and how relaxed people are and think we are near the end.

However, today for the first time in nearly seven weeks, it felt like a beautiful and normal day. I let my mind run away from me, thinking I was far away from here. Imagining that the beautiful weather I was soaking in was on some tropical island in some distant land where the virus cannot reach. My skin has absorbed the rays of the sun, my mind used the glow and brightness to distort the emptiness and blackness until they were so far away, I could no longer see them. Maybe I am just as bad as everyone else.

Day Forty Five.

Thursday 7th May 2020

Total UK Deaths: 539 Running total is now 30,615

Confirmed Cases: 206,715

- A spokesman for Boris Johnson says the changes in England next week will be "very limited." He also said Mr Johnson will be using "maximum caution" when starting to ease some of the lockdown measures which have been in place now for seven weeks.
- Scotland's First Minister Nicola Sturgeon however believes the lockdown in Scotland "must be extended" and easing any restrictions would be "very, very risky." She would like all four UK nations to work in unity and change any restrictions in tandem.
- In more embarrassment for the Government, the 84 tonne of PPE which was flown in from Turkey, eventually after a series of delays, cannot be used because it doesn't meet UK safety standards.
- The Bank of England expect the UK GDP to fall 14% this year due to the coronavirus, its worst annual slump for over 300 years. The bank also gives out warnings of the deepest recession on record.
- The Government are passing the blame to the coronavirus test labs after failing to reach its testing target of 100,000 tests per day, for the fourth consecutive day. Simply described as "technical issues" no detailed reasons have been given for such a dramatic failure.

Another strange day of feeling like I'm in limbo as the country sits back and awaits news from the Government. It's expected things will just go on as is until Sunday, but surely, they have to release a statement to say so.

Nothing can change until some lockdown restrictions are lifted, no plans can be made, and nothing can be put in place. I'm sure after so long people would like a little bit of insight into where we go from here.

The last volunteer got back to me last night, her work circumstances have changed, and she is now working a lot more hours, so can no longer commit any time to us. It's a shame to lose somebody, but I appreciate her honesty.

The weekly gift aid claim was completed this morning, raising £240.63. Although the figure has dropped dramatically, it is to be expected as I am now doing weekly applications. It's also still fantastic people are still making donations which we can claim on, despite everything which is going on. If we do get through all this, the support from the public will have had a major part to play. Something we will all be extremely grateful for.

I'm about to drive to Rothbury now, to catch the Post Office for the books which were sold. The optimism and enthusiasm of the sales and yesterday's sun drenched escape seems to have rode away into the sunset which brought a new dawn.

Quite a mundane day, but as I said there is an essence of being in limbo and treading water until we hear from Boris Johnson. I guess it is just typical of these very strange times.

Footnote: I don't know whether I should laugh or cry at this, but having made way to Rothbury to post the books, I arrived to find the Post Office (which is located in general dealers) has changed its opening hours and actually closed at 2pm. A perfect example of how this pandemic has affected the simplest of routines and how businesses must be struggling to continue to operate. I can feel the pressure rise inside my temples from such a simple inconvenience.

From a purely selfish point of view it leaves me in limbo again as to when these books will be posted. Tomorrow is a bank holiday for VE Day, after which I will be at work for three days.

Such an ordinary task has suddenly become hard work and a pressure of which I am struggling to comprehend. Why would a Post Office close at 2pm? Surely during this crisis, mail is the most important form of communication? I know the staff will say they are protecting themselves, and I fully accept and understand this, but it is just another very gentle and inconvenient reminder of the mess we are in. Driving back with my parcels I can't stop shaking my head.

I can only imagine how this is causing disruption to bigger and more powerful business, which in turn is why there is this massive push to get things back to normal. The frustration is immense, but we are all in the same boat. Yes, we all want things back to how they were, we want to get our lives and freedom back, but at what expense?

If I could save posting my books until a time when everyone was safe, I would. The big outside world has to put everyone's safety first, I understand that, but it feels as if we are not only playing roulette with people's lives but also people's sanity.

Day Forty Six.

Friday 8th May 2020

Total UK Deaths: 626 taking the total now to 31,241

Confirmed Cases: 211,364

VE Day.

- Celebrations are muted, but Britain still remembered the fallen on the 75th anniversary of the end of the second world war. A two minute's silence lead by Prince Charles at 11am, toast to the veterans at 3pm and the Queen to address the nation at 9pm.
- Once again, a warning comes from the Government to resist going out in the nice weather and to stay at home despite the Bank Holiday VE day celebrations.
- A six week old baby dies in the UK from coronavirus.
- The number of tests done in the last 24 hours is just over 97,000. Still short of the governments daily target.
- Environment Secretary George Eustice says there will not be any "dramatic overnight change" and the UK is "not out of the woods" during the daily press conference.
- Wales announce they will stay in lockdown for another three weeks, but restrictions will be eased slightly on Monday. First Minister Mark Drakeford announced three changes which will come into effect next week. They are: People will be allowed to go outside more than once to exercise, but it must begin and end at home and must not include travel. Garden centres can reopen as long as they adhere to social distancing guidelines and local authorities will begin to plan how to safely reopen libraries and tips.
- Whilst Australia sets out plans of a three stage process to lift the country's lockdown and restart the economy by

July. Under the first stage, restaurants will be allowed to reopen but with a maximum of ten customers at a time. If no major outbreaks of COVID-19 arise then the country will move to stage two. This includes gyms, cinemas and galleries to also reopen but again with a limit of customers. These establishments will be allowed twenty customers at a time. At this point, with the state borders shut, some interstate travel will be allowed. The third and final stage would allow gatherings of up to 100 people, allow staff to return to their offices and the reopening of nightclubs. All interstate travel will also be allowed, with some international trips too.

It was a strange feeling this morning checking the news to see the headlines dominated by something other than the decimation being caused by coronavirus.

It seems as if the whole country has decided to take the day off from the desperation and loneliness of isolation and all sorts of virtual parties have been taking place across the whole country.

The Red Arrows have flown over London, the Queen has given her speech, all things which have taken people's mind off what is going on for the first time in seven weeks.

Wales and Australia announcing ways in which they are looking to come out of this pandemic is also very positive and offers a glimmer of hope in all of the darkness.

Then there is the shocking news of the six week old baby dying from COVID-19. A harsh and brutal reality check in the midst of all the celebrations and a reminder of whilst we are not at war with another nation, we are living through a time which presents its own callous killer. One which is silent and holds no soul precious. A reaper so brutal even an infant of just six weeks is prey, and easy prey at that.

Day Forty Seven.

Saturday 9th May 2020

Total UK Deaths: 346 taking the total to 31,587

Confirmed Cases: 215,260

- Failure once more for the Government, as the total of tests for coronavirus conducted falls short of target again at 96,878. Seventh day in a row they have failed to deliver what they have promised.
- The British public are once again accused of ignoring restrictions during sunny weather. On Friday, HM Coastguard reported the highest number of call outs since lockdown began on Friday with 97 separate incidents. Which is a 54% increase on a normal April daily average. Whilst a Hackney Police statement posted on Twitter, with an image alleged to be of London Fields, said "Sadly we're fighting a losing battle in the parks today. Literally hundreds of people sitting having pizza, beers, wines."
- Cumbria Police share several examples of motorists who have been caught making non-essential journeys this Bank Holiday. One driver was stopped driving from Manchester to Dundee to buy a puppy. Another driving from London to Manchester to buy an Audi, then decided to drive to Cumbria to buy some speakers off eBay. A family from Wigan were caught 'out for a drive' to Windemere. Another had travelled 307 miles from Southend-on-Sea to the Lakes. On Friday, three men have travelled from Stockport to Cumbria "to feed the ducks."
- More than 2,100 nightclubs, bars and discos in South Korea's capital have been shut down after 18 new coronavirus cases. All but one of which could be linked to one 29 year old man.

- Police in London made a number of arrests and issued fines after breaking up an anti-lockdown protest near Westminster Bridge. Protestors brandished banners with messages including "no consent" and "we will not be tricked, tracked and trapped."
- Mark Adams, Chief Executive of social care provider Community Integrated Care claims the UK "are down to about 24 hours' worth of PPE."
- It is rumoured Garden Centres in England will be allowed to open from Wednesday as part of the first measures of reducing lockdown constraints.
- The Dementia UK helpline reports calls have risen by 44% during lockdown. In March this year 2,114 calls were made to the helpline compared with 1,464 in the same month last year.
- In Belarus, the military parade to commemorate the Allied victory over Germany in 1945 goes ahead despite the advice of the World Health Organisation. Thousands of soldiers marched past stands filled with onlookers. Dressed in military attire and shaking hands with all he met, President Alexander Lukashenko states he had no choice but to hold the parade.

Throughout this book I have tried very hard to state the events of what has been going on across the world, based on facts and actual events. I accept some of my political views will have become evident at times, for which I do not apologise, as somebody once said in a book title, I am only human.

As we are less from twenty four hours from Boris Johnson giving the most important announcement of his life, in some ways even more than the one he gave seven weeks ago, I am disillusioned and in total shock at the ignorance and total lack of common sense which has been displayed by people from every walk of life in the news stories above.

I am worried, I am concerned for the safety of my family, my friends and myself when such a self-destructing attitude runs through the veins of this country and across other parts of the world.

The UK is nowhere near ready to lift restrictions, society still hasn't conceived the severity of the situation which we are all facing, even after seven long weeks. I hope the Prime Minister has the strength not to submit to peer pressure and to do his job in protecting the people. If not, I fear the death toll will rise higher than our worst estimates and we will be in this situation for a long time to come. Wave after wave of infection and lock down, months and months which turn into years and years of limited life. The only way we can stop this happening is by facing up to what is going on around the whole world. The struggles and disruption all seem so harsh and intrusive right now, but in the long term they will save so many lives, maybe even my own. I understand the desperate need to get the economy going again, money makes the world go around, but as I close for the day and take myself off to the retreat and feeling of safety which only my bed can bring in these times, I ask you one more thing. Money does make the world go around, way more than love, faith and devotion, but during these times at what price?

Day Forty Eight.

Sunday 10th May 2020

Total UK Deaths: 269 taking total to 31,855

Confirmed Cases: 219,183

- The UK's death toll in the last 24 hours is the lowest since the 29th March (214) which was also a Sunday. Sometimes the figures at the weekend don't give a true reflection.
- As the Government misses its own target of 100,000 coronavirus tests per day for the seventh consecutive day, news comes of 50,000 test samples which have been flown to the US because of "operational issues" in the UK.
- Another Brighton & Hove Albion footballer tests positive for COVID-19, the third from the club to do so, highlighting the danger of restarting the Premier League season.
- Seven people have been arrested after police were coughed on and spat at whilst breaking up a birthday party that broke lockdown conditions. Around 40 people, including children were present at the party in Bolton.
- Boris Johnson addresses the nation with a "conditional plan" from the Conservative Government to begin reducing lockdown measures. The pre-recorded announcement was aired at 7pm and had the whole nation waiting with bated breath.

"It is now almost two months since the people of this country began to put up with restrictions on their freedom – your freedom – of a kind that we have never seen before in peace or war.

And you have shown the good sense to support those rules overwhelmingly.

You have put up with all the hardships of that programme of social distancing.

Because you understand that as things stand, and as the experience of every other country has shown, it's the only way to defeat the coronavirus - the most vicious threat this country has faced in my lifetime.

And though the death toll has been tragic, and the suffering immense.

And though we grieve for all those we have lost.

It is a fact that by adopting those measures we prevented this country from being engulfed by what could have been a catastrophe in which the reasonable worst case scenario was half a million fatalities.

And it is thanks to your effort and sacrifice in stopping the spread of this disease that the death rate is coming down and hospital admissions are coming down.

And thanks to you we have protected our NHS and saved many thousands of lives.

And so, I know - you know - that it would be madness now to throw away that achievement by allowing a second spike.

We must stay alert.

We must continue to control the virus and save lives.

And yet we must also recognise that this campaign against the virus has come at colossal cost to our way of life.

We can see it all around us in the shuttered shops and abandoned businesses and darkened pubs and restaurants.

And there are millions of people who are both fearful of this terrible disease, and at the same time also fearful of what this long period of enforced inactivity will do to their livelihoods and their mental and physical wellbeing.

To their futures and the futures of their children.

So, I want to provide tonight - for you - the shape of a plan to address both fears.

Both to beat the virus and provide the first sketch of a road map for reopening society.

A sense of the way ahead, and when and how and on what basis we will take the decisions to proceed.

I will be setting out more details in Parliament tomorrow and taking questions from the public in the evening.

I have consulted across the political spectrum, across all four nations of the UK.

And though different parts of the country are experiencing the pandemic at different rates.

And though it is right to be flexible in our response.

I believe that as Prime Minister of the United Kingdom – Scotland, England, Wales, Northern Ireland, there is a strong resolve to defeat this together.

And today a general consensus on what we could do.

And I stress could.

Because although we have a plan, it is a conditional plan.

And since our priority is to protect the public and save lives, we cannot move forward unless we satisfy the five tests.

We must protect our NHS.

We must see sustained falls in the death rate.

We must see sustained and considerable falls in the rate of infection.

We must sort out our challenges in getting enough PPE to the people who need it, and yes, it is a global problem, but we must fix it.

And last, we must make sure that any measures we take do not force the reproduction rate of the disease - the R - back up over one, so that we have the kind of exponential growth we were facing a few weeks ago.

And to chart our progress and to avoid going back to square one, we are establishing a new Covid Alert System run by a new Joint Biosecurity Centre.

And that Covid Alert Level will be determined primarily by R and the number of coronavirus cases.

And in turn that Covid Alert Level will tell us how tough we have to be in our social distancing measures – the lower the level the fewer the measures.

The higher the level, the tougher and stricter we will have to be.

There will be five alert levels.

Level One means the disease is no longer present in the UK and Level Five is the most critical – the kind of situation we could have had if the NHS had been overwhelmed.

Over the period of the lockdown we have been in Level Four, and it is thanks to your sacrifice we are now in a position to begin to move in steps to Level Three.

And as we go everyone will have a role to play in keeping the R down.

By staying alert and following the rules.

And to keep pushing the number of infections down there are two more things we must do.

We must reverse rapidly the awful epidemics in care homes and in the NHS, and though the numbers are coming down sharply now, there is plainly much more to be done.

And if we are to control this virus, then we must have a world-beating system for testing potential victims, and for tracing their contacts.

So that – all told - we are testing literally hundreds of thousands of people every day.

We have made fast progress on testing – but there is so much more to do now, and we can.

When this began, we hadn't seen this disease before, and we didn't fully understand its effects.

With every day we are getting more and more data.

We are shining the light of science on this invisible killer, and we will pick it up where it strikes.

Because our new system will be able in time to detect local flare-ups – in your area – as well as giving us a national picture.

And yet when I look at where we are tonight, we have the R below one, between 0.5 and 0.9 – but potentially only just below one.

And though we have made progress in satisfying at least some of the conditions I have given.

We have by no means fulfilled all of them.

And so no, this is not the time simply to end the lockdown this week.

Instead we are taking the first careful steps to modify our measures.

And the first step is a change of emphasis that we hope that people will act on this week.

We said that you should work from home if you can, and only go to work if you must.

We now need to stress that anyone who can't work from home, for instance those in construction or manufacturing, should be actively encouraged to go to work.

And we want it to be safe for you to get to work. So, you should avoid public transport if at all possible – because we must and will maintain social distancing, and capacity will therefore be limited.

So, work from home if you can, but you should go to work if you can't work from home.

And to ensure you are safe at work we have been working to establish new guidance for employers to make workplaces COVID-secure.

And when you do go to work, if possible do so by car or even better by walking or bicycle. But just as with workplaces, public transport operators will also be following COVID-secure standards.

And from this Wednesday, we want to encourage people to take more and even unlimited amounts of outdoor exercise.

You can sit in the sun in your local park, you can drive to other destinations, you can even play sports but only with members of your own household.

You must obey the rules on social distancing and to enforce those rules we will increase the fines for the small minority who break them.

And so every day, with ever increasing data, we will be monitoring the R and the number of new infections, and the progress we are making, and if we as a nation begin to fulfil the conditions I have set out, then in the next few weeks and months we may be able to go further.

In step two – at the earliest by June 1 – after half term – we believe we may be in a position to begin the phased reopening of shops and to get primary pupils back into schools, in stages, beginning with reception, Year 1 and Year 6.

Our ambition is that secondary pupils facing exams next year will get at least some time with their teachers before the holidays. And we will shortly be setting out detailed guidance on how to make it work in schools and shops and on transport.

And step three - at the earliest by July - and subject to all these conditions and further scientific advice; if and only if the numbers support it, we will hope to re-open at least some of the hospitality industry and other public places, provided they are safe and enforce social distancing.

Throughout this period of the next two months we will be driven not by mere hope or economic necessity. We are going to be driven by the science, the data and public health.

And I must stress again that all of this is conditional, it all depends on a series of big Ifs. It depends on all of us – the entire country – to follow the advice, to observe social distancing, and to keep that R down.

And to prevent re-infection from abroad, I am serving notice that it will soon be the time – with transmission significantly lower – to impose quarantine on people coming into this country by air.

And it is because of your efforts to get the R down and the number of infections down here, that this measure will now be effective.

And of course, we will be monitoring our progress locally, regionally, and nationally and if there are outbreaks, if there are problems, we will not hesitate to put on the brakes.

We have been through the initial peak – but it is coming down the mountain that is often more dangerous.

We have a route, and we have a plan, and everyone in government has the all-consuming pressure and challenge to save lives, restore livelihoods and gradually restore the freedoms that we need.

But in the end, this is a plan that everyone must make work.

And when I look at what you have done already.

The patience and common sense you have shown.

The fortitude of the elderly whose isolation we all want to end as fast as we can.

The incredible bravery and hard work of our NHS staff, our care workers.

The devotion and self-sacrifice of all those in every walk of life who are helping us to beat this disease.

Police, bus drivers, train drivers, pharmacists, supermarket workers, road hauliers, bin collectors, cleaners, security guards, postal workers, our teachers and a thousand more.

The scientists who are working round the clock to find a vaccine.

When I think of the millions of everyday acts of kindness and thoughtfulness that are being performed across this country.

And that have helped to get us through this first phase.

I know that we can use this plan to get us through the next.

And if we can't do it by those dates, and if the alert level won't allow it, we will simply wait and go on until we have got it right.

We will come back from this devilish illness.

We will come back to health, and robust health.

And though the UK will be changed by this experience, I believe we can be stronger and better than ever before. More resilient, more innovative, more economically dynamic, but also more generous and more sharing.

But for now, we must stay alert, control the virus and save lives.

Thank you very much."

Day Forty Nine.

Monday 11th May 2020

Total UK Deaths: 210 taking the total to 32,065

Confirmed Cases: 223,060

- Britons are now being asked to wear face masks on public transport and in shops where social distancing is not possible. After weeks of insisting there was little scientific evidence to support the fact face coverings were effective in protecting people from coronavirus, the Government are now recommending the public make their own using an old t shirt and elastic. The advice is included in the Government's 50 page document entitled "Our Plan to Rebuild: The UK Government's COVID-19 Recovery Strategy" which has been released after the Prime Minister's speech last night.
- The first morning after the announcement sees the London Underground packed full of commuters, many of whom are not adhering to the social distancing rules. Photographs taken by an anonymous tube train driver shows people crowded together with shoulders touching and very few wearing face masks.

Absolute confusion is the only way I can describe the state of the UK as I wake this morning. The words from Boris Johnson last night seem to have caused absolute havoc within the community, with nobody really sure about what they can do or what they should be doing anymore.

From the charity's point of view, I quickly arranged a video call meeting between the three trustees to thrash out exactly what information needs to be passed onto the staff and volunteers. My phone was busy all morning with people asking can they come back now they were allowed. I have a different opinion from what was broadcast, but I need to see what Joan and Jon think too.

During the meeting it all became clear none of us think it is safe to relax our own restrictions just yet. Joan raised a very good point with the VE Day celebrations on Friday, and the lack of respect of the social distancing rules, there could be a huge rise in cases in a couple of weeks times.

So many streets had parties where crowds were supposed to be staying in their own gardens, but of course after a few drinks people dropped their guard. Joan witnessed this in her own street, kids all playing together, people wandering around and sharing drinks.

We decide it is in the best interests and safety of the staff and the two volunteers who have joined the teams, we continue with our lockdown practice for another three weeks at least. We know this will upset people, but we must put the welfare of the dogs first which means making sure the people who look after them are as protected as we can possibly make them.

We also decide during this three week period we will start to make firm plans on how we go forward after lockdown, prepare our own recovery plan if you like.

There is so much to consider, from how we bring the two teams back together again, how we integrate the volunteers and of course, how we manage to get the shop open again and meet the safety procedures.

I end the call with my head buzzing. We have so much work to do just to try and get back to a position of normality. It is going to be stressful and difficult. One thing I have learnt from all of this, is you cannot please everyone, and I must make decisions which I think are the best for our dogs. I expect staff to be unhappy about the extension of the reduced hours (I understand their feelings and appreciate the sacrifice they are making) and I expect volunteers to be frustrated at once more not being allowed to return to the kennels, I understand that too, but if we can stay safe for just a little bit longer then we can start addressing both of the above and hopefully become a better functioning organisation.

Thirteen years ago today, the organisation you all now know as SHAK, made perhaps its first major rescue. Back then it was just me, I was working in a kill shelter desperately trying to save as many as I could from the vet's needle. I wasn't the easiest of employees, nor was I afraid to stand up for the dogs. Especially the ones who were doomed to be murdered by people who hadn't spent days looking after their victims.

Like every organisation, the orders came from the top. Management made decisions on lives simply by listening to stories or looking at dates on kennel records to see how long an animal had overstayed its welcome.

One day I was feeding a dog in the stable block which was being used as an overflow area. I heard a noise in the stable next door and went to investigate. A beautiful, strong looking Lurcher had been placed there and was clearly waiting for his evening meal. I went and sought management to find out his story and to see if he needed fed. Their reply had me in shock.
"Don't worry about him, he's getting destroyed in the morning." Was what I was told.
"No, he is not." I replied, "he's in one of my kennels now." Before disappearing to go and prepare him some tea.

Toffee, as he was called, didn't get destroyed the next day. He had been brought back to the pound for suffering from separation anxiety, a crime he had committed several times before.

I managed to persuade the 'powers that be' to allow me to work with him for a while, he was the dog who began my love of sighthounds.

The occasion was the first time of three the people above me pushed to take Toffee's life. He was probably only about two at the time and just a couple of months earlier he had been the pride of the place in the local press, having his photograph taken with a national hero, Johnny Wilkinson who had just returned from winning the rugby world cup with England.

The third and final attempt was the straw which broke the camel's back. Sitting in the staff room listening to my manager try and justify the names on the list which were to be butchered in their pre-summer cull, I told her in front of the dozen or so staff, it was "bullshit." I removed my works t shirt; with name of the place I had come to despise emblazoned on the front and threw it in her direction. At which point I wheel spun my car out of the car park.

Not the most professional way to deal with a situation I disagreed with, but it was complete frustration at how they could value a life at so little. A quarter of a mile up the road I realised what a mistake I had made. How had I been so foolish and selfish. If I wasn't there to protect him, they'd kill him for sure. I spun around in a bus stop and made my way back. I apologised for my behaviour; said I would accept any punishment they wanted to dish out. I had no respect for their management, organisation or morals, but I was positive they wouldn't break me. I also told my manager before vet's day; Toffee would be well gone from this wicked place.

In the space of about forty eight hours I had arranged to get my chest waxed. I spoke to everyone I knew and managed to raise the £100 adoption fee which was needed to buy my mate out of the pound and off death row.

Somebody arrived to look at dogs the day before the vet was due. Surprisingly, they took an instant like to Toffee and were more than happy to part with £100 to make him part of their own family.

Watching as he walked out of the place which was intent on killing him with his 'new owner' made me realise I had to keep on with this fight. Toffee looked so proud as he strode towards the car, he never once looked back at me. He was just relieved to be out of there, never knowing just how close he had come to losing his life. My manager glared across the yard as he left, confused but also with a little hint of respect in her eyes. She knew what I'd done. Deep down I think she quite liked it.

After a brief spell in kennels until I was able to sort him a permanent home, along with another lady in rescue called Alexa who has helped me ever since. Toffee went from facing the needle to living in some of the most beautiful places in Northumberland. Embleton, Bamburgh and Rothbury were all on his list of the places where he went on to love his freedom. I lost contact with his owners several years ago, I expect he will have finally moved onto Rainbow Bridge by now, but I know he had a great life. One which was so cruelly nearly taken from him so many times all those years ago. I guess you could say he was where all this really started.

Day Fifty.

Tuesday 12th May 2020

Total UK Deaths: 627 taking the total to 32,692

Confirmed Cases: 226,463

- Ironic now the weekend is behind us, the death toll has almost tripled from the figures given out on Sunday and Monday. I also found it very strange the Prime Minister gave his announcement on Sunday rather than the previous Thursday, which was when the original three week period of lockdown expired. Forever the cynic, could this have been so as he talked about lifting certain restrictions the death figures were at their lowest for a long time?
- The Governments furlough scheme, which supports 7.5 million workers, has been extended until the end of October.
- Health Secretary Matt Hancock declares summer is cancelled after appearing on ITV's This Morning. When asked the question outright whether the British public will be able to holiday abroad this summer or is it cancelled, he replies "I think that's likely to be the case. It is very unlikely that big, lavish international holidays are going to possible this summer." Adding "I just think that's a reality of life."
- Matt Hancock has also denied the Government's new coronavirus guidance is confusing, urging the public to apply the "straightforward" rules with "common sense." For his example he now claims that people can meet a different person in the park every day, although they must stay two metres apart. Although he did later admit such behaviour was "not zero risk."

- Northern Ireland's government has published its own five stage plan for gradually emerging from the coronavirus pandemic. However, unlike Boris Johnson's confusing plan, this one is not governed by time, but will be reviewed every three weeks. The message is simply "Stay home, save lives." In phase one, groups of four to six people who do not share a household will be allowed to meet outdoors, whilst maintaining social distancing. People who are unable to work from home will be encouraged to go to work on a phased basis. Large outdoor based retailers, such as garden centres, will be allowed to reopen. As will drive through cinemas. Eventually, by phase five, large indoor gatherings, nightclubs, concerts, contact sports, restaurants, café, pubs and early year education will also be permitted to operate.
- Wuhan, the Chinese city where it is believed coronavirus originated, now faces another crisis. Lockdown measures, that were in place from 23rd January, were lifted on April 8th. However, today they have announced every one of their 11 million citizens will now be tested, after six new cases were recorded over the weekend. There have also been new outbreaks in the city of Shulan and South Korea, all of which gives strength to the argument this disease will raise its ugly head in waves.
- A mother working as a ticket collector in London, has died from COVID-19 after being spat at by a member of the public claiming to have coronavirus on the 22nd of March. Belly Mujinga (47) was working on the concourse at Victoria Station, London at the time of the attack.
- The Department of Transport have issued new guidance on how to travel on public transport, after the photo's emerged yesterday of the shambolic scenes on tube platforms throughout London. Passengers have been told they should avoid eating and drinking whilst travelling,

- and they should face away from other passengers when there is not enough room to social distance. Given the intensity of the congregation in the photographs from yesterday, the latter seems both impossible and ludicrous to suggest.
- Footballer Danny Rose, who is currently on loan at Newcastle United from Tottenham Hotspur has today's last word though. In a world where the pressure seems to mean pound notes mean more than lives, the full back delivered the following message in a live interview on Instagram "I don't give a fuck about the nations morale, bro, people's lives are at risk. Football shouldn't even be spoken about coming back until the numbers have dropped dramatically."

So, after the confusion and need for some kind of stability yesterday, the work begins today in trying to pave our own path to recovery.

Just before all this kicked off, we had secured funding to hire a manager to run the retail side of the charity, as well as opening a second shop. Jon had secured the premises in the seaside town of Amble and we had also found the man to steer the ship in our, soon to be, new shop manager Geoff. All we were waiting for was the shop's refurbishment to be completed and the lease to go through all the legal hoops that these things have too. Then coronavirus rocked up.

Everything has been on hold since the original announcement by Boris Johnson fifty days ago, only today, the people who have the reigns of the charity under their control, took the first steps of trying to rebuild.

Geoff, Jon and Joan all researched and discussed the complications involved in reopening one shop and opening another. There is so much red tape and legislation regarding social distancing, we are going to have to make some significant changes to how 'SHAK Retail' operates.

Geoff's position has obviously been put on hold, as at the moment he has no shops to manage, but today he has offered to work a month as a volunteer to try and re-establish our trade and to look at moving the new shop to a position where it could be ready to open. Working alongside Joan to inherit the knowledge of what has been a very successful and amazing job done in Blyth, Geoff hopes to be able to help us keep our volunteers and customers safe and the latter spending.

Due to being over 70, my mam is limited to what she can physically do because of the Government's restrictions, another issue we will have to address as a lot of volunteers in the shop are over 70, but hopefully they can work something out.

It has to be said Joan and her team have done an amazing job in the Blyth shop and created a secure platform for us to go forward on. Her forced retirement is a hard one for her to take, but I think I can speak for all of us when I say that without her hard work and dedication, the charity wouldn't still be here. I'd like to thank her and every single member of her team for taking us this far.

Jon's other half Sandra is also a very valuable asset, as a retired accountant. She has been a huge help with doing the accounts, but also during this crisis by providing regular cash flow forecast's and making sense of all the numbers. Today she has been looking into another powder keg which is holidays, as a couple of the staff are querying how the new working conditions will affect their holiday accrual. I'm not sure it is something which would be high on my list of concerns given the international pandemic, but I guess people are worried about their own positions and have families to consider, again something I appreciate. The worry is understandable, and something which as an employer, we need clarity on.

Whilst everyone else has been beavering away, I too have been heavily engrossed in administrative work, as I plan the rota's for how we all start to integrate together again after our self-imposed lockdown procedures expire.

I have to consider how we merge the two teams and what is the best days to do various tasks, I also need to look at how volunteers can fit into the pattern, so everyone remains safe.

In my working week I want two days to be different from how it has been in the past. This lockdown has proven how important it has been for me to have a day where I can catch up on all the administration duties which come with my role in the charity. In the last seven weeks or so I have raised just short of £25,000 with carefully worded appeals which were published at just the right time, I have raised media awareness of our plight with BBC Radio interviews and newspaper coverage, I have claimed over £5,000 back in gift aid claims. Without any of this, it is debatable whether the charity would have survived, meaning it has to be questioned whether our dogs would still be alive.

I am not saying this to 'blow my own trumpet,' but it is a fact when I started doing this fourteen years ago, it was all my own initiative, Toffee's story proves this theory. I enjoy steering the ship, I feel I am good at doing all of the above and to take the charity on further I need to go back to basics and spend more time doing it.

Through all of their hard work, the staff have proved they can still get the dogs out with a minimum of three people in all day. The way it was before the pandemic, meant I felt guilty if I ever took time away to do these jobs and leave the staff 'shorthanded.' If I hadn't made this step during lockdown, there would be no staff. They wouldn't have jobs to keep, I need to make sure I make space to spend my time productively and hopefully be able to raise the money which will improve working conditions for everyone.

So, from now on in, I will have a specific administration day each week. This will allow me to look at all kinds of ways to increase awareness, revenue and managing the people involved with us.

Secondly, I have also noticed by working with every dog in our care for three days a week, as opposed to just the most difficult, I have reconnected with them and learnt a lot about where they are in their lives. Some of it good, some of it bad. This in turn has highlighted some areas which I know I can work on and hopefully help them go on to find homes in the future, or at least be a little more stimulated on a day to day basis.

This will include taking them to different surroundings for assessment and seeing exactly what they are like away from the kennel environment. I am looking at ways to use the sensory room more, enrichment areas and more one on one time. All of which is the reason I do this work.

I have come up with the term 'Practical Days' and I intend to also use them to help train staff and volunteers in body language, handling techniques, calming signals etc. All the things which I have learnt the hard way and would benefit the dogs on a daily basis if they were used by more people.

I see the emergence out of this crisis as a new start and one which will allow me to hit the 'reset' button and regain the determination which saved Toffee's life thirteen years ago.

I look at what we have achieved since that day, right up to recruiting Geoff and the second shop, and I am very proud, but like everything in this world we need to change to progress and to continue to survive. Evolution rather than revolution, as Charles Darwin once said, "It is not the strongest of the species that survives, nor the most intelligent, but the ones most responsive to change."

Day Fifty One.

Wednesday 13th May 2020

Total UK Deaths: 494 taking the total to 33,186

Confirmed Cases: 229,705

- Labour leader Sir Keir Starmer accuses Boris Johnson of misleading Parliament about Government advice which stated people in care homes were unlikely to catch coronavirus.
- Buses were packed and people enjoyed games of golf and tennis, as the lockdown measures were reduced from today. Very few people on public transport were wearing facemasks or able to stay two metres apart. The RMT transport union warn public transport workers are worried about the conditions and services may need to be stopped to keep people safe.
- Building sites are to increase their hours of work late into the evening, as part of the Governments bid to restart the economy. Mondays to Saturdays they will be able to operate until 9pm in residential areas, whilst they can work even later in non-residential areas, Communities Secretary Robert Jenrick announced today.
- The NHS contact tracing app which is currently being trialled on the Isle of Wight, is experiencing some serious issues with its software Downing Street has revealed. Heralded as an important part of the country's recovery from COVID-19, it is the latest setback facing the Government.
- Spain is planning to open its borders to holiday makers from early July. Austria and Germany, both of which went into lockdown early in the pandemic, are scheduling their borders to open on the 15th of June.

- As today is the first day of the UK slightly reducing its own restrictions, Birmingham City Council mow two metre strips into the grass in their parks to help with social distancing.
- The Chancellor warns the UK faces a significant recession, as figures show the economy shrank by 2% in the first three months of the year.

Another day of number crunching and go back and forth via email. We (the Trustees) have decided as we were planning to restructure the holiday procedure anyway, the best way of trying to look after all the staff is, we change our holiday year to start from the first of July. To avoid any complications with this, the charity will pay staff for the holiday they have accrued between the first of April, when our leave year currently starts, and the first of July.

During the deepest trench of lockdown, we offered the members of staff who were losing hours because of the three on, three off schedules, the chance to take paid leave so their wages weren't affected. As it happens, no holidays were taken, so by getting the holiday pay backdated it should in theory make up for some of the shortfall.

The shop has played a massive part in the charity's survival and it essential we get it open as soon as we can but also, we need to be sure it is a safe environment for both volunteers and the customers. Joan has been in discussions all day with volunteers who have made the Blyth shop the success it is and Geoff. They have all arranged to meet next Tuesday, obviously adhering to social distancing rules, to look at the layout of the shop floor and see how they can effectively implement the same safety measures once it is open.

The slight changes to the rota which I have been working on has also been approved by the other trustees. Essentially the purpose of these changes is to allow me to carry on the work which has been so successful during Lockdown. We aim to implement the new two weekly rota on the first of June, as it seems to be the date which is being brandished about for things getting back to normal. From there on in I will have an admin day in the office and a 'practical' day, where I do what I need to do more of, actually work with the dogs on a one to one basis.

There is so much going on behind the scenes preparing for when we hopefully can all come out of this. I'd like to thank everyone for all their hard work. When this is all over, I hope the staff, volunteers and our supporters can read this book and see just how many hours of hard work have gone into our survival, by so many people.

We have all had to try and learn things, we have all had to be patient and do so much research. We have grown as a management committee; we all need to continue such growth to see the job through. I know my head hurts trying to comprehend how we can all pull this together, but it is without doubt something which we have to do.

All it needs is a fresh outbreak of the virus and the whole country is back to square one.

Day Fifty Two.

Thursday 14th May 2020

Total UK Deaths: 428 taking the total to 33,614

Confirmed Cases: 233,151

- Statistics from NHS England show a quarter of the people who have died with coronavirus in English hospitals had diabetes. People with dementia or lung problems were next on the list. The figures show 22,332 (26%) of victims who have died since 31st March were diabetic, although it has not been revealed whether they had type 1 or type 2. 18% (4,048) of the deaths were people which had dementia as an underlying health condition, whilst 15% or 3,214 of the total had chronic pulmonary disease. A further 3,214 (14%) had chronic kidney disease.
- An updated estimate from the Office of Budget Responsibility regarding the cost to taxpayers of the Government's response to the coronavirus pandemic, has jumped up from £103.7bn to £123.2bn.
- Reports state Mexico City is on the brink of a coronavirus disaster due to its poverty and weak health service.
- Researchers have found using ordinary mouthwash could be effective in stopping the transmission of coronavirus in its early stages of infection. The research, led by Cardiff University, examined whether mouthwash could damage the outer lipid (fatty) membrane which envelopes the virus, and therefore inactivates it.
- Peter Brown, director of Forest Road Brewery Co has begun a great operation for those of us missing being served a pint in the pub. Putting as many kegs in his van as possible, which he has rebranded a "tactical beer response unit" he sets off around the doors of Hackney

delivering freshly poured pints to your doorstep. Obviously sticking to social distancing guidelines and wearing a face mask, one customer said this about Peter, "The man is a hero, simple as that. Not all heroes wear capes, but this man should."
- A primary school headteacher in Kent has written to the parents of every pupil in his school, asking them to ignore Government advice and not to send their child back to school on the 1st June, as social distancing would be "impossible." In the letter, Howard Fisher states he would "rather a child repeats the year" than die.
- People visiting A&E departments in England have fallen to their lowest figure on record, as people choose to stay as far away from hospitals during the coronavirus outbreak.

On the last point, I have to say I fully understand. After the incident with Bobby a few weeks ago I really should have gone to hospital to be checked over and get antibiotics.

Over the years I have been doing this I have been bitten so many times I know when it is serious enough to warrant the long waits in hospital and the endless number of repeat visits for dressing changes and checks.

The bites I received that day were bad, but it wasn't even the thought of all the valuable time being wasted which put me off dropping into Alnwick Hospital, it was the fear of exposing myself to people and this hideous virus.

Today I had to go to the Post Office in Rothbury again, this was my first day out since yesterday announced the arrival of slacker restrictions. The difference was noticeable from the off.

Fencers, builders and men in unmarked vehicles, all either hogged the road or were pulled in various laybys and fields. It was just after twelve and they were nearly all on their lunch. Sitting in the cabs of their transit vans and pick-ups, social distancing has gone out of the window.

I arrive in the small town itself and again the tranquillity and calm which has been evident on all of my previous visits on my shopping trips here, has been violated.

Motorbikes are parked in the spaces which have been readily available for the last seven weeks. The park benches are full of leather clad men drinking from bottles of soft drinks, I have to walk around one group just so I can get to the post box safely. Its both unnerving and intimidating.

The man who runs the local post office is a character. I don't even know his name, but the last few weeks have seen me get to know him well enough that I am comfortable enough to engage in conversation with him when I visit. Last time it was about dogs who don't like dog food. My old Greyhound, Sky, has taken a like to such delicacies as meatballs and ravioli. Having been vegetarian for over thirty years before becoming vegan two years ago, buying such processed death is something I find uncomfortable at the least.

However, she is fourteen and has beaten cancer once. The weight has dropped off her over the last twelve months. Right now, she can eat anything she wants too.

Anyway, the man from the post office was telling me how his dog is similar but as long as he pours some of the tomato sauce from a tin of baked beans on its food, he will eat anything. A tip I bear in mind, today I bought Sky a couple of tins of beans and sausages.

Today's conversation was a little dourer. We were talking about how the place seemed busier and trying to decide whether it was a good thing or not. I could tell he was weighing me up and looking to see just how far he could push this.

"It's very good for the economy" he said, then he paused. "But once people are mingling, the virus could go boom again." He stopped and stared at me, then a look in his eyes indicated he felt he could trust me.

"It's all down to common sense" he starts "the people who come in here are mostly ok. They are very careful, but some of them" the pause again, before he continues "some of them, you wonder how they actually got themselves ready in the morning."

With that his parting shot, we laugh, and I make my way to exit. Then I remember one of the reasons I called in, wasn't to buy sausages and beans, it was to pick up a birthday card for my stepdad Mike.

Going back towards the far end of the shop, I leave the postmaster to entertain the queue of people which has formed behind me and head towards the birthday cards.

I pick one which mocks the birthday boy for supporting a team that rarely wins, being a Manchester United fan Mike hasn't had a lot to shout about for a few years, then I take my place at the back of the queue.

Making sure I stay at the yellow markers on the floor which indicate two metres, I eventually get to the till to see the same guy I had the conversation with two minutes earlier repeatedly sanitising his hands on wipes and with gel.

"What were we saying before?" he says, a huge frown creeping across his face like a big black ugly cloud which is determined to block out the sun on a summer's day, just as you've lit the barbeque.

"Thought it was a good idea to lick his fingers as he counted out his money." The look in both our eyes is enough. Returning to the Land Rover, I get my own spray sanitiser out of my pocket and spray it all over my hands and the wrapper of the birthday card.

On returning home, I message my mam to tell her I have posted Mike's card. I am hopeful that six days should be enough time for it to make the eighteen mile journey, even in these terrible times.

The conversation progresses to Rothbury, bikers and both of our worries the Government have been too soft and lifted restrictions for financial reasons rather than considering the safety of the public.

Then she sends me a screenshot of a news article she has been reading. It is a day or two old, but the message is clear. I looked it up myself before I started writing todays entry.

The articles I find all say the same thing, cases of coronavirus in Germany have almost trebled in a twenty four hour period, less than a week after the nation's lockdown restrictions were relaxed.

Health authorities have reported more than 900 new cases have been recorded in that period. A real worrying figure and one I fear I will be reporting on in this book regarding our country.

The charity has said throughout the whole of this pandemic, we are working to government guidelines. By looking to reopen the shop and merge the two teams of staff, as well as looking to begin to integrate volunteers from the 1st of June, I have to say I am apprehensive.

We all need things back to the way they were. We all need to start making money and ease the pressures not working brings. We all want this to be over.

What I've witnessed on something as simple as a trip to a small rural town's Post Office, fills me with dread though. If the Government have got this wrong, who will be held responsible? Whose fault will it be, the law makers or the people which fail to abide by the laws which they have set?

I'm sitting outside in broken sunshine, with Sky lying at my feet. I don't think it is my company she is after; I think she is waiting for me to stand up and prepare her sausage and beans!

I guess the answer to the blame question doesn't really matter though. If the country suffers a second spike in this killer, then everyone will be responsible. The politicians, the public, the police. People will die, that is for sure, when maybe staying sheltered for just a couple more weeks will have saved some of those lives.

Day Fifty Three.

Friday 15th May 2020

Total UK Deaths: 384 taking the total to 33,998

Confirmed Cases: 236,711

- The R is a measure of how fast coronavirus is spreading. Above 1 an outbreak is growing, below 1 it is shrinking. It is estimated using data from hospital admissions, intensive care demand, deaths and the number of social contacts people have. The R number has risen over the last week according to The Scientific Advisory Group for Emergencies. The new figure is between 0.7 and 1, an increase from 0.5 to 0.9 last week. A coincidence with lockdown measures being eased.
- The daughter of a man who died of suspected coronavirus in a care home in Oxfordshire, has called the government's policies "irresponsible" after untested patients were sent into care homes. Dr Cathy Gardner fears that the policy could have been a factor in her 88 year old father Michael Gibson's death.
- The NASUWT (Teachers Union) has said a meeting about reopening schools on the 1st of June, has "raised more questions than answers."
- Every person prosecuted under the Coronavirus Act was wrongly charged, the Crown Prosecution Service has said. Officers are allowed to remove or detain a "suspected infectious person" for screening and assessment under the Act. However, all 44 charges brought up until the end of April were classed as incorrect.
- The five stages in Ireland's plan to unlock lockdown restrictions will begin on Monday. Taoiseach Leo

>   Varadkar warns "there will be bumps in the road" as they look to implement the stages at three week intervals.
> - The number of people becoming infected with coronavirus each day in London may have fallen to 24, but the North East of England sees around 4,000 new infections a day, new research shows.

The last statement confirms my fears, as I still believe restrictions are being lifted to quickly and to soon. Throughout this crisis the North has been a few weeks behind the South, which has almost made some people up here complacent. If people think everything is beginning to clear, they may not see the danger creeping north.

At the kennels, today seems to be harder work than normal. I can't quite put my finger on why, but I can feel the stress levels beginning to rise the moment I arrive.

Behind the scenes we are working so hard to try and make the adjustment back to some form of normality as easy and as safe as possible. This of course, means I have an abundance of phone calls, messages and emails to respond to, as well as doing my share of the day to day work. Once again, the pressure I feel under is beginning to feel a little too much.

Gemma, our friendly dog warden who we work so closely with, swings by to drop of some boxes of dog waste bags. We have a quick catch up from a distance of well over two metres in the opposite end of the farmyard to the kennels. She is on her way to another rescue, with a beautiful German Shepherd who has behavioural problems.

I'm not sure how the other rescue is able to operate so they can still take new dogs in, but I guess it is good they have somewhere to go. If we were to take in new residents it would probably tip the whole thing over the edge. Such is the sensitivity of the situation.

It hurts like mad though. I founded the charity to be able to take in dogs like the one in the back of her van. German Shepherds especially, as they are my breed. I feel frustrated and sad. We may still be here and looking after the very special dogs which we have, but we are failing others. No matter how much I try and forget about it throughout the day, it just leaves a sting in the back of my throat.

Once again, Emily the vet, shows how much the charity means to her by being on the end of the phone. Tommy, a nice Staffy Cross, is passing blood when he urinates. I send photos and converse with her over the phone. She agrees it may be a UTI (urinary tract infection) but also says it could be something more sinister. She recommends we try a course of antibiotics for five days to see if there is any improvement. If not, we'll need to get him in for scans and further investigation. She offers to take the medication home for me to pick up on my own journey home. A service which once again is above and beyond the call of duty and so vital to our dogs in this climate. We are all very grateful.

Day Fifty Four.

Saturday 16th May 2020

Total UK Deaths: 468 taking the total to 34,466

Confirmed Cases: 240,161

- Education Secretary Gavin Williamson has sought to reassure parents and teachers worried about the Government's plans to get some children back to school on the 1st of June. Speaking at the daily briefing he said the decision was based on the "best scientific advice" and they had put children at the heart of their decision.
- National Park visitors surge despite the Government's plea to stay away. In only four days since Boris Johnson announced people could have a little more freedom, it seems people have completely ignored what has been going on for the last eight weeks. On Friday night a group of eight people were handed COVID-19 fixed penalties in the Dales for camping out, whilst North Yorkshire Police announced they had found a group of travellers together from six different households. Low fuel costs and nice weather, coupled with what I still consider a ridiculous decision by the Government, means an expected 15 MILLION drivers will head onto our roads this weekend.
- Two months after the season was curtailed by coronavirus, football in Germany and the Bundesliga is back. In a ground-breaking development for sport, the games are played in empty stadiums, whilst the players adhere to social distancing guidelines when they score. In rather ironic scenes, Borussia Dortmund's players salute the fans after a 4-0 derby win against local rivals Schalke. Only the terraces they are celebrating in front of are empty.

During the last bit of advertising for It's A Dog's Life I received an order for a copy from Dominic Hodgson. Dom is a well-known dog behaviourist who I met when he chose us to be one of the stops on his Tour De Rescue bike ride last summer. A really nice guy, he seemed to fully understand the role we play in the dog world, and more importantly he was very supportive of the reasons why.

I sent his book out a few days ago then, last night, he posted a picture of himself holding it on all his social media with the words "Just got this delivered. It's ace Steve Wylie."

I messaged him this morning to say thanks for promoting it and for the support. His reply left me speechless and made me very proud.

"It's topper mate. Seriously impressed. I'm putting together a little free eBook for Kindle around rescue dogs, how to settle one I, like a little training tips anthology, I'm getting my dog trainer pals to donate a chapter each. Be great for you to contribute sometime if you want. Even a chapter of that book would do. Would get a bio about you and SHAK with a call to action to go and donate to SHAK after your chapter. No pressure at all, I know that you are mega busy, but I'm doing it anyway, would be great to involve you somehow if you like."

In all this darkness and worry, it's a great feeling knowing somebody who has so much experience with dogs and their behaviour has been touched by something which I wrote all those years ago. Even more so that my style of writing has impressed him enough for him to want to include some of my work in a book of his own.

After work and sorting all the animals out here, I sat with a vegan pizza, a glass of beer and started working on a small piece which I think will cover what he is looking for. I've no idea how it will go, I just write what comes into my head. I decide to give what I have written so far, the working title of 'Home.'

At the kennels today it was all hands on as usual. The necessity of getting the job done, means I haven't been able to do as much with the dogs over the last two months as I would have normally done. They haven't been neglected as such, just my role has been very similar to everyone else's.

Today I decided I wanted to introduce Tia to Axel. Both German Shepherds with a little bit of an attitude, something in my head just said to give them ago.

It was really interesting watching them weigh each other up at first. Rachel had Axel, I had Tia. He was interested, she was snappy. He ignored her; she was interested. I watched them both throughout the walk, observing all the body language and the calming signals which were now flowing in both directions, then on the way back I took both leads and walked them together myself.

Seeing them together and figuring out what was going on between them gave me a real buzz. It made me realise what we do is special and how much I am actually missing doing it. Yes, we are surviving, which is the most important thing, but we owe these dogs more than that. They need our help, which is why they are here. The sooner we can start giving them it in greater quantities the better.

Today also sees the huge announcement to the staff and volunteers about what has been going on in the background, before lockdown and during it.

Jon sends out messages to everyone telling them about the appointment of Geoff and how close we are to having a second shop. It all seems to be well received, in fact some people comment on how exciting it all is and share the vision of it making us more self-sufficient.

Sharing the news fills me with excitement and nerves, but also reiterates the need to get back to normality and how things were. I am beginning to feel frustrated and tired with the conditions we are operating in and being unable to do my job to the best of my ability. I know it is the same for a lot of people, but as we are about to enter Mental Health Awareness week, I do worry for myself and about how we are all going to recover from this very difficult time.

Day Fifty Five.

Sunday 17th May 2020

Total UK Deaths: 170 (Of course this is another Sunday) taking the total to 34,636. Also, the lowest amount of deaths since the 24th March.

Confirmed Cases: 233,151

- Spain announce their daily coronavirus death toll has dropped below 100 for the first time in months. A total of 87 people died in the last 24 hours. In another story, the Spanish transport minister has said the country aims to open its borders to foreign visitors by late June, as the country tries to make the most of the summer season in an attempt to kick start its economy.
- The new relaxed rules allowing people to travel anywhere for leisure purposes, have already started to cause chaos on Britain's streets. The police in Helmsley, on the edge of the North York Moors National Park, were called out half a dozen times yesterday because of congregations of bikers visiting the area. Tensions created out of fear and frustration by local residents, the vagueness of the Government's stance must once again be questioned.
- A rave in Telford attended by around 70 people was shut down by police, in a blatant lack of respect for rules and for others. The party goers claimed they were "sick of self-isolation." Police were said to be shocked and urged anyone thinking of arranging any similar events, to think of the bigger picture.
- Antony Cauvin, a 29 year old plasterer from Stratford-Upon-Avon, has made the headlines by inventing "the Cuddle Curtain" so he could hug his grandma. Made from a shower curtain with pairs of safety sleeves on

either side, the invention allows two people to stand immediately in front of each other and hug.

Today started like every other day on my team's shifts of three in at the kennels, but by the end of it we were all very flat and dejected.

One of the sights which has kept me going over the months of lockdown, has been seeing Oscar make his way around the field in his wheelchair, sniffing the air and taking in the fabulous views of the Northumberland countryside. Not once did he look like he didn't want to go out, nor did he ever look bored. In fact, I think he lived for his duty of his own close down last thing at night. He knew he was the final walk of the shift, checking the gate was shut for another day and making sure the field was secure, meant his job was done.

He came to us about nine years ago. He had shown some serious aggression towards people, especially when being touched around the head by his owners, who were old school colleagues of mine. They had two young twin babies; the risk was just too much for having an unpredictable dog in the house. The first time they asked me to take him, we didn't have room. So, they went and tried everything they could. Behavioural sessions, training classes, they even bought him a treadmill to try and work off some of the abundance of energy and tire him out. The second time they asked me they were desperate. The babies had begun to crawl and pull themselves up on things, Oscar was getting grumpier by the day and they were worried if either child decided to pull themselves up on him, he would react.

As it happened, I had just rehomed a big Rottweiler called King, so I had a kennel free this time. Oscar arrived the very next day.

He was as strong as an Ox and very sure of himself. The story was he had been split from his mother at five weeks old and then spent the first few months of his life being passed around various homes until my friend took him in. He was four when we got him, they had tried so hard for three and a half years.

I believe the reason behind his behaviour and self-confidence; was mainly down to the fact he had been separated from his mother too early. He had been shown no boundaries, had no rules installed, nor been told biting was inappropriate. Instead he found his own way through life by being confident in his own ability to protect himself, demanding in getting what he wanted and just an all-round determination and strength his breed is capable of.

Over the years he was with us, he mellowed slightly. I used to walk him with some of my own German Shepherds, I think he quite liked Star, whilst his tolerance of people and touch also improved.

He loved playing with his boomer ball and had a great trick of collecting up to four tennis balls in his mouth at one time. There was no way he was ever going to let you take any of those. I think he was happy with us and grew into kennel life. He didn't feel under any pressure, so we began to see the real Oscar.

As he grew old his back end begun to let him down. The German Shepherd curse of Canine Degenerative Radiculomyelopathy (CDRM) struck, but it couldn't keep him down. He still managed to get out and about, a little wobbly, but it didn't stop him enjoying his walks.

When the condition grew worse, we integrated a rear harness to help support him. Calling them his "Super Hero Underpants" they took some getting on, as the procedure included lifting his rear legs through holes, just like putting on underpants, then handles so the handler could hold up and offer support to his back legs.

At first the reaction from him was what we all expected. We used a muzzle to keep us safe, but very quickly he realised we were trying to help him. After a couple of weeks, the muzzle was discarded and getting him out in such a way just became a fact of life.

Oscar's condition got worse by the end of last summer, which meant fewer people could walk him because of the weight and strain it put on the handler's shoulders. It was a horrible feeling because so many people loved him, mainly for his attitude, but were now unable to spend time with him.

I had a few sleepless nights trying to think of how we could help him, each time my mind kept returning to the same obvious answer.

Years ago, we had the biggest German Shepherd I have ever seen in Doyle. He too suffered from CDRM and we managed to extend his life by about six months by using a set of wheels which had been donated. Over the years since we had taken in another set, but they just looked so complicated when trying to get a difficult dog in them.

One Saturday I watched somebody struggling to walk him and decided enough was enough. We had to do something to help Oscar and we had to understand he would react, and it wouldn't be easy.

Myself, Rich and volunteers Paul and Mick volunteered for the job of trying to get him in the wheelchair which Doyle had loved so much. I got it out of storage and tried to adjust the straps so it would comfortably fit Oscar, as Doyle was so big.

The muzzle came back out, which was just as well, as we quickly found out there was no way that Oscar was going to allow us to restrain him in such a contraption.

The design of the chair meant he almost sat on his rear hunkers and used his front legs to pull himself along. We eventually got him in it, but he was stressed. He walked around the farmyard for a little while but was very unhappy. He would have bitten if he wasn't muzzled and we all knew this wasn't the answer we were looking for.

Dejected and upset, the four of us stood and looked at each other. Nobody said anything. We all knew if we couldn't make this work, Oscar's time with us wouldn't be much longer. It wasn't fair to him to leave him struggling, but nobody wanted to mention the idea of putting him to sleep.

"Let's go and walk others and think." I said, desperately trying to clear my head and come up with a moment of inspiration. It was Paul who had it.

I returned to the kennels to find Paul had got the other wheelchair out and was trying to figure out how it worked. This one was different as instead of sitting in it, the dogs back legs slip through two rings and hold up the back end. It was just like Oscar's underpants, only on wheels.

I gathered the guys together again and suggested we tried once more but using this different chair. Everybody agreed, so out came Oscar and the muzzle.

He adored it right from the off. He struggled at first to allow us to help him in, thank goodness for a five pound muzzle is all I'll say, but once he realised he could go where he wanted again and as fast or slow as he wanted, he was in his element. He even learnt he could reverse and sniff a bit he had missed. The change in him was sensational and something which I will never forget for as long as I am involved with dogs.

That Saturday afternoon changed Oscar's life, but also extended it until today. The muzzle became a thing of the past very quickly and now there was a queue of people wanting to get him out again. He had his independence back and was always in such a hurry to get out once he saw you approaching his kennel with his wheels.

There was a look in his eyes of pride and determination. This wasn't a disabled dog who was feeling sorry for himself, this was a dog who knew he had a second chance at going all the places he wanted to. He could give the boomer ball holy hell again; he could do treat searches on his own. He could do what he wanted once more.

Although he had begun to look a little tired of late, Oscar wasn't one for giving up. This morning Rachel had him out for his survey of his grounds as usual. He ate his small treat which he always demanded as reward on his return then settled down, content at watching everything else which was going on around him and in the kennels.

He always watched, which was the benefit of him being in the kennel right at the front. If anything was happening Oscar let you know, but for me personally it was always the fact he knew exactly where I was and what I was doing which will stay with me. The sight of him lying on his huge mattress, chin flat on the surface but those eyes taking everything in and following you around.

It was because he wasn't in such a position this morning as Rachel passed, she thought something was wrong. She called for me and I went straight over to see him. I instantly shared her concern and knew something wasn't right.

He had turned away from the front, positioning his body so he was facing the back wall. My heart sunk as there is no way Oscar would have normally done that. Then I noticed the shape of his abdomen.

Swollen and rock hard, there was only one thing this could be, a GDV (Gastric Dilatation Volvulus) or stomach torsion. Within minutes he was in the back of Rachel's car and we were on the way to Emily the vets once again. Due to his condition and other ailments we all knew this was the one which was going to beat him. It would be unfair to put him through the massive surgery and to be honest I don't think his body was strong enough to withstand the anaesthetic never mind the surgery itself.

There were tears as I pulled away, knowing I wouldn't be bringing him back. The noises echoing from the boot meant I knew I had to get him there as soon as possible.

Several times on the journey, Oscar sat up and looked at me directly in the rear view mirror. His eyes had a deep and knowing look about them. I kept telling him we wouldn't be long and to hang on so Emily could check him over, then he would lie down again.

The tree in Emily's back garden now has become a place I will never forget. Just a few weeks earlier Rachel and I had said goodbye to Sheba in glorious sunshine as the birds sang, in the exact same spot as I was standing again.

Today the skies were grey, and the rain made it feel like the clocks had been turned back to February. Because of social distancing I couldn't hold him, but Oscar knew I was there.

As he slipped away, he turned and looked at Emily, then back at me. He looked at her once more, then turned towards me and put his head down like he always did. His beautiful eyes absorbed everything which was going on around him for the last time, then he closed them.

Oscar was a dog which gave us all inspiration. His determination and bravery meant he never gave in. The fact he adapted to being helped and understood his life depended on it, showed he had learnt to trust. The number of friends he acquired through displaying such trust means we all have been left with a huge hole in our hearts.

He had become such a big part in the daily routine of so many people, it really will be difficult to accept he is gone. I know however, he wouldn't want us to be upset and moping around, it just wasn't his style. He would want us to show the same fighting spirit he had throughout his life, he would want us to show such determination and make sure we get through this very difficult time, just like he did. It is that thought I will carry around with me forever.

Day Fifty Six.

Monday 18th May 2020

Total UK Deaths: 160 taking the total to 34,796

Confirmed Cases: 246,406

- The UK records its lowest daily coronavirus fatality figure since the nationwide lockdown began.
- The Health Secretary announces anybody over the age of five who displays coronavirus symptoms, are now eligible to be tested for the virus.
- The loss of taste and smell are being added to the Governments list of coronavirus symptoms. Medically known as anosmia, the condition joins the list where people suffering should self-isolate, along with a continuous cough and a fever.
- Bars, cafes, shops and restaurants have reopened in Italy today after being closed for over two months because of lockdown restrictions. Hairdressers, churches, museums and beaches also reopened.

Today is just flat. Trying to absorb what happened yesterday just seems to have amplified the feeling of hopelessness and frustration which living in lockdown has produced.

I am full of mixed emotions. I want things back to normal, but still think it is too soon. I want the best for our dogs, but I am struggling to see a way we can bring everybody back together safely without taking risks.

I popped into Alnwick shopping earlier, it was almost as if nothing was going on. People were ignoring the two metre rule, there were crowds on the streets. I am not going to hide the fact I am frightened about what will happen. I am worried and feel under immense pressure to make decisions and to get them right. The stress is beginning to take its toll once more, but on an even bigger scale.

Then my mind drifts back to Oscar and everything I wrote about him yesterday whilst fighting back the tears. He was a fighter and a survivor, I said we should all learn from him and follow his lead. I must take note of my own words.

I don't know whether the feeling physically sick permanently is down to grief, shock or stress. Or whether it is a combination of all three, but I can't shake it off.

I can feel the cracks beginning to show, I can feel myself beginning to drown in the pressure of it all.

Day Fifty Seven.

Tuesday 19th May 2020

Total UK Deaths: 545 taking the total to 35,341. However, the Government also release figures which show the total of deaths which mention COVID-19 on the death certificate is actually 41,020

Confirmed Cases: 248,818

- More than 11,600 people have died in care homes across the UK since the start of the Corona virus pandemic figures suggest.
- Professor Jonathon Van Tam warns COVID-19 may return in the autumn and winter as the virus may come in waves.
- Captain Tom Moore is to be given a knighthood after raising £39 million for the NHS

Today I made my write up on Oscar public, putting it on our website which automatically shares it onto Facebook and Twitter. The reaction was immediate, with people who didn't even know Os reduced to tears. I also had to tell his former owners we have lost our boy.

It's a strange feeling once the news is out there. It feels like the darkness which has shrouded me since the shock and horror of Sunday morning has gone, but the bitter taste of loss and grief remains.

I have tried to remain positive, taking the inspiration I keep talking about from the fabulous dog which we have all just lost, but it simply isn't so easy.

Since lockdown started, and after they published my initial appeal, the Northumberland Gazette have disappeared off the face of the earth in terms of supporting us. I have sent them articles for our very successful column, they haven't printed them. I have emailed the editor and all the reporters who I have worked alongside over the last 3 years, none have replied. I don't know why; the paper has been very thin in both substance and content in the last few weeks. Maybe they are struggling like us all. Still, it appears very ignorant and rude.

So, doing what Oscar would do, this afternoon I have emailed the Chronicle, which is Newcastle's biggest daily newspaper, then sent an amended email to every national newspaper that I can find contact details for.

I don't expect anything to come from any of it. We are such a small organisation, the emails probably won't even be read, but at least I have tried. I haven't given in.

Oscar's death has made me think about a lot of things. The way we operate, what we do, how the world can know about what we do. The admin days which I have given myself in the new rota pattern will be paramount in our existence and growth. Having the desire to start by sending out these emails today is a massive step forward for me mentally if nothing else.

Day Fifty Eight.

Wednesday 20th May 2020

Total UK Deaths: 363 taking the total to 35,704

Confirmed Cases: 248,818

- A world beating track and trace system to stop a second coronavirus peak and help ease the lockdown has been promised by Boris Johnson to be in place by the end of May.
- £150m from dormant bank and building society accounts will be unlocked to help charities and social enterprises affected by the pandemic.
- NHS Medical Director Professor Stephen Powis states that for the first time since March, there are now fewer than 10,000 people in hospital with the virus, with 9,953 patients currently in care.

The UK has wallowed in the hottest day of the year so far, unbelievable temperatures and a glorious change to the mixed bag of wind and rain which we have had to deal with over the last week or so.

Today is the last of my three away from the kennels, so I have to admit I have submitted and treated it like a day off, one which I think I desperately needed.

The temperature here has gotten up to 22 degrees. Something which I can't remember ever happening before, it has been just like being abroad, or at least from what my long lost memory tells me anyway.

That doesn't mean nothing has been done though. We have all had moments finalising plans for the new shop and the reopening of the existing one. After the meeting yesterday between Joan, Geoff and some of the volunteers from Blyth, which apparently went very well, it appears that the reopening is pencilled in for the 8th of June.

Jon and volunteer Mick have started acquiring the PPE and items which are required for the shop to finally open its doors again, something which is close but also so far away.

It all seems so long ago, since the little hive of activity provided the hub to our very existence. It will be good to start getting it back to that kind of level again.

Day Fifty Nine.

Thursday 21st May 2020

Total UK Deaths: 338 taking the official total to 36,042

Confirmed Cases: 250,908

- I've just been looking back over my figures for confirmed cases on the 19th and 20th of May and they are the same? I apologise, I have been searching the web for the last hour and I can't find a different figure. Sorry.
- Boris Johnson has pledged to scrap the fee for foreign health and social workers "as soon as possible."
- During the Governments daily briefing, Health Secretary Matt Hancock reveals a coronavirus test which will deliver the results in twenty minutes, is currently being trialled. The new test does not need to be sent to a laboratory to be processed, so will ease the worry of the public who have had to wait days or even weeks for the results.
- In the same briefing, Matt Hancock also announces coronavirus antibody tests will be available on the NHS. The Government have signed an agreement with pharmaceutical firm Roche and Abbott to provide 10 million kits, which in turn will show if somebody has had COVID-19 and potentially developed an immunity to the virus.
- The Scottish Government have announced a five phase "route map" to relax lockdown restrictions, which will be reviewed every three weeks. The new rules are expected to begin on the 28th May are: People will be allowed to sit and sunbathe outdoors. People will be able to meet one person from another household, if they stay two metres apart outdoors, including in gardens. Visits inside another household are not allowed. Non-contact sports

- like golf, fishing, bowls and tennis will be allowed. People will be able to travel, preferably by walking or cycling, to carry out activities, but they should stay close to home. Recycling and waste services will resume. Garden centres will be allowed to reopen. Some services like social work, will resume, as will some parts of the criminal justice system.
- Reports state thousands of coronavirus test results conducted by the Governments main testing lab, are coming back classified as "unclear." Adding to the stress and worry of needing tested in the first place, this means people then face another wait to be retested. According to Sky News, 4% of swab tests conducted at the Lighthouse Laboratory in Milton Keynes, are classified as "unclear" because of the limitations in the chemical testing process.
- Finally, more than five million people worldwide have been infected with coronavirus, whilst over 328,100 have died. These figures reported by the John Hopkins University.

Although I wasn't at the kennels, I kept in touch with how Tommy was doing. I don't know if it was because what had happened with Oscar, but I was worried. Naomi, who is the volunteer on the other shift, has a real soft spot for him. I knew she would keep a close eye.

She reported he was still passing blood when he urinated, but it wasn't congealed like the discharge we had seen on our shifts. He had just finished his antibiotics, but I had a gut feeling we needed him checked over, even if it just served to put everyone's mind at rest. I spoke to Emily, who agreed if that was how I felt, then he should go in.

Her practice has started doing a little work, but the owners still aren't allowed in the building. As soon as I mentioned it to Naomi, she offered to take him and pay the bill, such is her love for Tommy. A fantastic and greatly appreciated gesture on both counts.

When I arrived at work this morning, there was no visible signs of blood in his kennel. I rang Emily and said as everything was arranged, we should still go ahead. I got Jax to help me get a fresh urine sample to accompany him, which was a job in itself. I have never known a dog kick his legs after urinating in such a fashion that he spills nearly every drop you have collected by hitting the dish! Still it proved to be enough.

I'd given Tommy a glowing reference, along with permission to muzzle if needed. He didn't let me down. No muzzle was needed to obtain blood for testing, whilst no sedation was needed for an abdominal scan. He was quite happy to let them do both.

The bloods showed his liver enzymes were slighted elevated, but the scans showed his spleen, kidneys, liver looked fine. Thankfully, the original diagnosis of a really bad UTI looked as if it was accurate. At least we know for sure now though, internally things are ok.

Having seemed to quite enjoy his day out, Tommy returned with another week's worth of antibiotics and instructions if we see no more blood in his urine by the time the medication is finished, then all we need to do is take him back in a month's time for more blood tests just to make sure the liver enzymes have returned to normal.

I can't tell you how relived I am, and I know everyone else will be just as relieved. For a spell I was worried we may be losing another of our boys, which simply does not bear thinking about. Tommy is a nice boy, who I think has had it tough in the past. The fact we can now look after him and provide the best care for him means a lot. Thank you, Emily, Naomi and Ivor.

Day Sixty.

Friday 22nd May 2020

Total UK Deaths: 351 taking the official number of COVID-19 associated UK deaths to 36,393.

Confirmed Cases: 254,195

- New arrivals in the UK will have to face a two week quarantine from June the 8th. Anyone who breaches the measure will face a £1,000 fine.
- The owner of Shearings, who provided coach holidays, crash into administration. The result of which is the immediate loss of 2,500 jobs and thousands of customers holidays cancelled.

Day sixty and still we have no direct feed of optimism from the Government. I understand in a way how difficult it is to motivate and lead, because the people involved with the charity are looking at the Trustees for answers, but nobody has been through this before.

Today when I awoke, I looked at the SHAK calendar hanging on my kitchen wall and realised how close the 1st of June is. The magical day when everything will start to go back to normal and people's lives will return to some form of normality. We have already advised the staff it will be the day we will be looking to integrate both teams of workers. Teams, I have to say, who have produced amazing results over the last 8-9 weeks. But it really isn't so simple.

Volunteers are a big part of this charity, mainly because we have never had reliable corporate funding to be able to support the financial burden which comes with employing the amount of people, we would need to run the place comfortably. Yet each and every single volunteer brings a skill and commitment to our cause, something we are very grateful for.

They give up their free time for nothing and do it for their love of our dogs.

Today I opened the door for two volunteers returning every day from the 1st June, but with one condition, they have to be able to do a full shift. It's not to be awkward or to make things difficult, but for the safety aspect and the actual work which sanitising between people brings. By allowing anymore volunteers through the door the whole procedure would just become more complicated and time consuming, as well as multiplying the risk to us all.

I expected an indifferent reaction from some, but hopefully people will realise we are making these decisions to protect people.

It's not easy having to tell people who adore coming here and love every single one of our dogs, only two of them per day will be allowed access. It breaks me just thinking of it to be honest.

"We know you have been missing the dogs, and what is more we know the dogs have been missing you.

It has been a hard slog getting all the dogs walked at least twice a day with the two teams, but all the staff have stepped up to the plate magnificently; we have achieved our objective and the two walk tally is currently sitting at 91 (will be 92 by the end of the day) but has been very hard work.

Boris has promised us an easing of the lockdown from 1st June, and assuming it does happen, we want to start reintroducing volunteers to the kennels again, but we must do that in a controlled and responsible way to keep everyone as safe as possible.

Our aim is to have two volunteers alongside the staff team every day wherever possible but not more than that. To reduce the need of sanitising and cleaning between shifts, we ask that the volunteer shifts must be either a full day or a minimum of 10-4. This protocol will be in place for the first three weeks.

Can you please message me directly and let me know what days you can be available in the week starting on the 1st June and we will try to put a rota together which achieves that end.

It is possible it may mean on some days we have more volunteers than we can accommodate, in which case some people will be on a reserve rota or on every other week or whatever, but for the time being we must insist people don't turn up to help unless they are on the official rota.

Thank you for being so understanding in these difficult times, this is for the safety of everyone."

The positivity of the fact we are looking forward and opening the doors, even if it is just slightly, comes with a huge influx of uncertainty too.

Society is becoming complacent in my eyes, but we have to look to what the Government are advising. I feel anxious at the decisions we are having to make, on every level, but I really don't know what else we can do. The world cannot stand still, we all have to learn to adapt and adjust to move things forward. I just cannot reiterate enough how important it is we do it safely.

On a positive note, there was no blood in Tommy's kennel this morning and it was reported on his walks it was all clear too. Such a relief and I think the support he has had in these desolate times, from the teams, Emily and Naomi and Ivor shows how much we all love him.

Day Sixty One.

Saturday 23rd May 2020

Total UK Deaths: 282 taking the total to 36,675

Confirmed Cases: 257,154

- Absolute outrage as it is revealed Boris Johnson's top aide Dominic Cummings travelled 260 miles from London to Durham, to stay with elderly parents during lockdown despite him displaying symptoms of coronavirus. Calls for his resignation or for the Prime Minister to sack him seem to have fallen on deaf ears, as a statement from Downing Street insist his actions were reasonable. "Owing to his wife being infected with suspected coronavirus and the high likelihood that he would himself become unwell, it was essential for Dominic Cummings to ensure his young child could be properly cared for." Number 10 said in a statement. Transport Secretary Grant Shapps later states "I can tell you the PM provides Mr Cummings with his full support." In a later news report, it is alleged Mr Cummings made a second visit to the family home on the 19th April.
- The University of Amsterdam has been studying the effects of four types of coronavirus for over thirty five years on ten different men. Today they claim a person could be re-infected within six months.
- As we approach yet another Bank Holiday which to most of us will be a non-event, Councils warn people against travelling to beaches and beauty spots, even though the temperatures are expected to rise.
- Brazil confirms more than 330,890 cases of COVID-19 meaning that it is close to overtaking Russia as the country with the second highest number of infections in

the world. A reported total of 21,048 coronavirus deaths, make it the hardest hit country in Latin America. Only the US, with over 1.6 million cases, has a higher figure.
- Car rental firm Hertz has filed for bankruptcy as people's movements ground to a halt during this worldwide pandemic. Court documents reveal the company plunged £15.3bn into debt, despite being allowed to still operate as an "essential business." Over 12,000 jobs have been cut, with 4,000 more workers put on furlough.

The allegations against Dominic Cummings have left me completely reeling today. After all the hard work myself and my teams have done to make sure we observe the Government's wishes, all the sacrifices people I know have made, the difficulties of being able just to survive and live, yet one of Boris Johnson's gofers believes he is above those conditions. What perhaps is even more infuriating, is the fact the Prime Minister, who claims he was close to death with the virus, supports his aide's actions and says he has done nothing wrong. What kind of example is any of this to set to a public who is already fragile and disillusioned?

Today was a very tough day at the kennels, as the weather seemed to fast forward to early October, with heavy rain and wind which nearly reached thirty miles an hour. It made the whole day even more difficult, considering the fact it was day three of three.

Still the team worked extremely hard and we all got through it, although you could see the tiredness etched on people's faces. Sheer exhaustion coupled with the stress of trying to adapt to the changes which are happening, the fear of uncertainty clouding the horizon. If things go to plan, we may only have one more stint like this to do. I am not sure how I feel about that.

The response to reintroduce volunteers from the 1st of June has been as well received as I expected, I guess. The full day criteria has obviously made it unfeasible for some, but hopefully we can get to the level of two volunteers per day for the full week.

I started making my own plans today too, as I started to analyse who my practical days should begin with. I'm thinking Dande and Casper at the moment, both for different reasons.

Dande is a young Romanian rescue who came to us just a couple of weeks before lockdown, after being taken to our vets to be destroyed by his owners. I had provisionally secured him a placement at another rescue, but obviously the fact the whole country has been closed down for months now, means it is an option which hasn't been pursued. I feel we can help him more ourselves now, start his life from scratch and see where we go. These days should allow me to take him away from the kennel environment and let me assess him a little more thoroughly in the outside world. My first instincts are he needs an experienced home, somebody who is used to dealing with a dog which has just reached adolescence, but he may show different traits away from here.

In Casper's case, I just want to see how he reacts away from the stress which obviously kennel life produces at times. I have a real soft spot for him, and have already told you his story, I want to help him because he really deserves something positive to happen for the first time in his life.

Day Sixty Two.

Sunday 24th May 2020

Total UK Deaths: 118 taking the total to 36,793 (the second lowest increase on a Sunday since lockdown began.)

Confirmed Cases: 259,559

- Transport Secretary Grant Shapps claims the stories Dominic Cummings broke lockdown regulations, not once but twice, are "completely untrue."
- Senior Conservative MP Steve Baker has a different opinion though, stating Cummings "should go." On a Sky News Sunday morning show, Mr Baker said, "he has at the very least not abided by the slogans that he has enforced on the rest of the country and that is why he should go."
- During the Governments daily briefing, Boris Johnson says Cummings "followed the instincts of every father and every parent" defending him further by stating his chief advisor "acted responsibly, legally and with integrity."
- The Royal Society for the encouragement of Arts, Manufactures and Commence (RSA) have suggested companies should split the workforce into two teams and work a split three day week, as part of the economic recovery from the COVID-19 crisis. A little bit ironic as we are now looking to move away from the exact same module, but also shows despite the disappointment from certain areas, we have been doing things right.
- The Government's test and trace programme is set to launch by the end of this coming week, after minister's recruit 25,000 contact tracers to carry out the scheme.

Back to house rest for three days for what could be the last time. It's a little bit of a strange feeling, the beginning of the end, but as I look to finalise the first rota involving volunteers, commencing the week beginning the 1st of June, my head hurts.

I now have enough volunteers to cover every shift in a partnership for the full seven days. Trying to make sure everyone understands things will be different to how it was before, coupled with the logistics of people getting in, makes it quite demanding, but safety is the utmost important element in all of this.

Anxiety and excitement at what could be a huge new chapter in the way the charity operates, the 1st of June could be the beginning of new beginnings.

Day Sixty Three.

Monday 25th May 2020

Total UK Deaths: 121 taking the total to 36,914

Confirmed Cases: 261,184

- The PM is facing even more pressure to fire his top aide Dominic Cummings. The campaign for his dismissal is now led by 17 Conservative MP's, Bishops and NHS staff. The Rt Revd Nick Baines, Bishop of Leeds took to Twitter to ask "The question now is: do we accept being lied to, patronised and treated by a PM as mugs? The moral question is not for Cummings – it is for PM and ministers/MPs who find his behaviour acceptable. What are we to teach our children? (I ask as a responsible father.) An NHS doctor working in a COVID-19 intensive care unit is equally disgusted. Dr Dominic Pimenta, a cardiology registrar, tweeted a picture of himself at work wearing PPE and stated "Frankly, Cummings spits in the face of all our efforts, the whole NHS. If he doesn't resign, I will."
- Elsewhere, Boris Johnson admits defeat, saying it will be "tough" to reopen schools at the start of June but has pledged to continue to work with councils to try and address the issue.

It's another beautiful day after three days of being battered by a wind which was quite unusual for this time of year. In the matter of hours, we went from sweltering in 22 degrees to 29 mile per hour winds. Just adds more fuel to the fire of these uncertain times. Life seems to be going from one extreme to another so quickly, in more ways than one. I know which one I prefer.

Sitting at the table on my patio, as the water gurgles through the old stone water feature, there is a calmness which was taken away by the winds. A comforting feeling as the sun bleaches down on the top of my head and shoulders, the smell of suntan oil and warm aroma of fresh coffee. Today it feels as if summer has come back again, the wanderer returning after too long away. I wonder if I will feel the same way about normality this time next week.

The thought of things returning to how they were means, I guess, my adventure writing this book is nearly over too. So far, sixty three days in a row, it has been my constant companion.

My time during lockdown has been very lonely, sharing what has been happening on a night-time, or during these days based at home, has given me a purpose and an outlet. During the long hard days at the kennels, running the thoughts through my head of what I was going to write when I got home, documenting the day's events and saying things over and over in my head so I wouldn't forget them until I got back to my desk and wrote them down, has all helped get me through the times I thought my body couldn't take anymore.

You'd be surprised at the moments when inspiration for the story lands, usually as one of the big boys like Jeff or Gunner is dragging me around the field. It's as if the hardship itself has been a test to see how much I wanted to finish this. The outcome was never in doubt, I just knew I had to.

There have been so many times when I wondered how it would end, both as in the demise of the world and the closing of literature, then I would just tell myself both will come naturally and when the time is right.

As we approach the promised land which the first of June will supposedly bring, it feels like maybe such a time is approaching. The end comes to us all eventually.

Day Sixty Four.

Tuesday 26th May 2020

Total UK Deaths: 134 taking the total to 37,048

Confirmed Cases: 265,227

- In a press conference at Downing Street Dominic Cummings faces the media to defend himself over the allegations of breaking lockdown regulations. During the interview he said he did not regret making the 260 mile journey and believes he behaved reasonably. He also confirmed after staying at his parents farm, the family of three then went for a "test drive" to Barnard Castle, 30 minutes away, to check if he was well enough to drive home 15 days after he had started showing symptoms of coronavirus. He added "My wife was very worried, particularly as my eyesight had seemed to have been affected by the disease. She did not want me to risk a nearly 300 mile drive with our child given how ill I had been."
- Cabinet Office Minister Michael Gove has defended Dominic Cummings, saying he was "wise" to make the trip to test his eyesight before making a longer journey. However, the trip also coincided with his wife's birthday and police chiefs have said if he was feeling unwell and his eyesight may have been impaired then he should not have been driving.
- Government minister Douglas Ross has resigned over the Cummings affair, piling even more pressure on Boris Johnson to sack his chief aide. In a letter addressed to the PM, Ross underlines the fact the he appreciates Cummings acted with the safety of his family at heart, he cannot justify his colleague's actions. "I have constituents who didn't get to say goodbye to loved ones;

families who could not mourn together; people who didn't visit sick relatives because they followed the guidance of the government. I cannot in good faith tell them they were all wrong and one senior adviser to the government was right."
- Boris Johnson announces outdoor markets and showrooms can start trading from June 1st, whilst all non-essential retailers, including High Street shops, can follow suit two weeks later on the 15th June. Employers will face spot checks to make sure they are implementing social distancing. Measures which will need to be taken to reassure staff and customers include: Placing a poster in their windows to demonstrate awareness of the guidance, storing returned items for 72 hours before putting them back out on the shop floor, placing protective coverings on large items touched by the public such as sofas and beds, frequently cleaning objects and surfaces which are touched regularly by people, including self-checkouts, trolleys, coffee machines and betting terminals.
- The latest figures announced from the Office for National Statistics show the number of deaths linked to coronavirus has fallen to its lowest level for six weeks. In the seven days leading up to Friday May 15th 4,210 deaths were recorded, the lowest since the week ending 3rd April when 3,801 were recorded. In total the figures claim over 47,300 deaths in the UK since the pandemic hit our shores.
- Tourists will be able to visit Spain from July 1st without having to quarantine for two weeks, although the Spanish Government has only mentioned reopening its borders to fellow European Union countries so far.

This afternoon was a really exciting moment for the recovery of the charity, as I finally got to meet Geoff and see the new Amble shop for the first time.

It is an amazing space and one which I can see really working. There is so much scope for display and stock, I could see in his eyes Geoff could see it too.

Jon has been so keen to secure this for us and he has worked so hard. I really believe he is right. The street was a hive of activity, even though the majority of the shops were still closed. Just people going about their business, but it is easy to see the potential of having a shop on that street would bring.

The meeting was attended by myself, Jon, Geoff and our friendly builder Ivor. Married to Naomi, I don't think he had any choice in getting involved with the charity, but his input over the last twelve months or so really has been sensational.

Fittings, floor coverings, signage, tills, posters, card machines, reopening the Blyth shop on the 15th June as per Government guidelines. Everything was discussed at a minimum distance of two metres. Surreal but very productive.

Whilst the black cloud is still hanging above us, it feels as if you look very carefully, between the dank, non-descript grey, you can see the glimmer and shine of the beautiful colours within the rainbow which is desperately now trying to take the sky for its own.

Day Sixty Five.

Wednesday 27th May 2020

Total UK Deaths: 412 taking the total to 37,460

Confirmed Cases: 267,240

- The Government's coronavirus test and trace system will be up and running tomorrow, according to Boris Johnson. Anyone in England who shows to have been in contact with someone who has been infected with COVID-19 will be asked to isolate for 14 days, even if they have no symptoms.
- As part of the system, Matt Hancock confirms localised lockdowns may be introduced if high increases of coronavirus are spotted in individual areas. "We will have local lockdowns in future where there are flare-ups," he announced at the latest Downing Street coronavirus briefing.
- A senior Police Commissioner has said people caught breaking lockdown restrictions are citing Dominic Cumming's behaviour as the reason why they are showing complete disregard for the rules. David Jamieson, the West Midlands Police and Crime Commissioner, states that members of the public are telling officers that "if it is okay for Cummings, it is okay for us."
- Continuing on with the theme of a Government which is beginning to bring shame on the country for the whole world to see, the family of Conservative MP Rob Roberts were, in his words, "reminded of the guidance set out by the Government," after police broke up an illegal birthday party at his house.
- Some NHS patients with severe coronavirus symptoms will be treated with an Ebola drug after trials proved it

led to a quicker recovery. Health Secretary Matt Hancock added the breakthrough was the "biggest step forward in the treatment of coronavirus since the crisis began."
- One million businesses have claimed a massive £15bn from the Government's coronavirus job retention scheme to cover the wages of the 8.4 million furloughed workers, official figures show.

Today I had to make a very sad phone call after learning a relative had lost a German Shepherd which she helped me save about thirteen years ago.

My Mam's cousin, Josie, had boarding kennels when I was growing up. She also showed Japanese Chins, tiny little dogs, which were pretty cute and wanted cuddles, but it was always the huge German Shepherds which she had to protect the place who grabbed my attention on family visits.

As a child, I loved going there, I genuinely think those visits unearthed my natural love for dogs, and the ability to understand them.

In her younger days, Josie was more than a match for the biggest GSD in size and attitude, despite being of tiny frame herself. In fact, the local police used to call her and ask her opinion (which always ended in "yes, I'll take it") when they had taken one into custody after it had gotten itself in trouble. You have to remember this was the 1970's and the 1980's, German Shepherds (or Alsatians as they were known then) had such a terrible reputation.

Nobody has ever said it out loud, but I do think somewhere along the gamily gene pool, I had a strain of what Josie had too.

The dog which I had to make the call about today, was a female German Shepherd which came into the pound where I worked when I started this journey all those years ago. The same one Toffee was in.

She was a stray, stressed to hell and the destruction order was placed on her head by the management pretty much as soon as she arrived. At that particular time, I had managed to talk the bosses, who never left the sanctuary and heat of their office, to let me place some of the bigger breeds with breed specific rescues. I'd managed to save so many Rottweilers, Greyhounds and of courses GSD's by building relationships with rescues, who had also grown to trust my judgement and assessment.

Things were going well, and the rescue partnerships were really making a difference, then I took Sadie to meet my contact from a Scottish German Shepherd rescue which I had been using for about the last six months. The rescue had taken maybe a dozen dogs from me, from big handsome males to a few oldies, we worked really well together. It was such a good feeling getting an intelligent breed out of the disheartening and lethal environment of the kill shelter, where any form of work or rehabilitation was never going to happen.

I transported Sadie in my own time outside of work hours, in my own car, to the usual halfway meeting point. Nothing prepared me for the desperate and empty feeling which was going to accompany me on the return journey.

The dislike between dog and rescue coordinator was like nothing I have ever seen before. The moment I got her out of the Mitsubishi Warrior I drove at the time, the lady from the rescue disliked her. Obviously, such an intelligent dog picked up on such a negative vibe immediately and showed the woman what she thought of her.

What followed next was a conversation about how German Shepherds with amber eyes were trouble. This lady had seen so many over the years and never met a nice one. Absolute bullshit and the mutual respect vanished with one sentence.

So Sadie was rejected, no consideration given to the fact when I took her back to the shelter when it opened in the morning, her life would be taken, no thought given to the fact each dog is an individual and deserves a chance on its own merit. If I had a similar view on people, I would be deemed a bigger bigot than Hitler and all the other idealists which have caused death and misery across the world.

I never used or contacted the rescue again.

None of which was a comfort though, none of it helped. I had a dog in the back of my vehicle which I knew would die if I took her back to the hell hole I worked in. As we made our way back down the A1 in complete silence, my head was all over trying to think of options, desperately attempting to manufacture a solution which would save Sadie's life. Then I remembered my Aunty Josie.

She was apprehensive at first but showing a spirit which I myself have come to adopt over the years, she said "bring her down, she can stay here for a little while."

Of course, I don't need to tell you what happened next. Unlike the encounter at Haggerston Castle, it was love at first sight, and as they both grew older together, the bond became unbreakable.

Despite her problems with strangers, and an unmistakeable lack of trust for anyone other than Josie, Sadie died earlier this week at the ripe old age of fifteen, after her back end went and she began to suffer.

Three wonderful German Shepherds we have now lost with the same problem since lockdown began. I am really lost for words to describe how I feel, and how I sympathise with others whose lives were touched by the dogs which we have been able to save from death after being discarded.

It all seems so long ago since the drive back in the dark with a dog who hated most people in the back of my car. I can still feel the panic which was racing through me as I knew unless I could come up with a plan, the next journey Sadie would make would be in a black bin liner.

I can still remember the surge of joy and hope which engulfed my body when Josie said to take her down to hers. I will never forget the hurt and pain in her voice today as she told me how the events of the last couple of days had unfolded. Pain mixed with a top heavy ingredient of pride. The little dog which nobody else wanted changed my Auntie's life forever.

If this story doesn't motivate me to carry on and show others there is an alternative, I really don't know what else any of us can do.

Day Sixty Six.

Thursday 28th May 2020

Total UK Deaths: 377 taking the total to 37,837

Confirmed Cases: 269,127

- Groups of six people from different households will be able to meet outside in England after the PM claimed all five tests to ease the lockdown conditions were being met. Speaking at the daily briefing, Boris Johnson announced the public would be allowed to meet in gardens and other private outdoor places from Monday.
- He also confirmed primary schools and nurseries will be allowed to reopen from the start of next week, with year 10-12 pupils getting "some face to face contact time" from June 15th.
- The Premier League will make its return on June 17th, three months after the season was put on hold after the outbreak of the coronavirus pandemic.
- Too much media space is now being given to the disgrace which is Dominic Cummings, it is clear the Government which is running this country dreadfully (in my opinion) is not going to do the honourable and right thing, so by giving it publicity it will only offend people with the same beliefs as me even more. This notion is compounded by the statement from Durham Police stating Dominic Cummings may have committed "a minor breach" of lockdown conditions by travelling around the country, but he will face no further action.
- As people lose more faith in the Government, Matt Hancock laughs off more claims the new coronavirus test and trace system was hurried out to take the heat off the aforementioned Dominic Cummings accusations.

- EasyJet to cut up to 4,500 jobs because of coronavirus crisis.

I am worried about all of the above even more than before, as it appears the whole country is relaxing into the fact this all over. I really don't think it is.

I have spent most of the day in between dog walks, trying to get the message out to the staff and volunteers how important it is they follow the protocol, which has served us so well for the last three months, once we begin to reduce our restrictions on the 1st June. It seems to get a mixed response, but again I will emphasise I am not prepared to put the safety and lives of the dogs at risk by making myself more vulnerable.

I am frightened everywhere I look; people are already beginning to socialise beyond the boundaries which have been set in stone for so long now. I understand the frustration at being separated from loved ones, I have not seen my family for over nine weeks, in which time I have seen my daughter once. We are all feeling the strain, but there are still nearly 400 COVID-19 deaths in hospitals in the UK every day. Which is such a frighteningly massive amount.

I really can't write anymore without losing my temper at the risk I feel the Prime Minister is putting us under by making the changes so quickly.

I, more than anyone, is really looking forward to working with both the dogs and the people on a nice, new clean canvas, but I am willing to wait until I feel it is right to ease things even more. I hope people understand that.

Day Sixty Seven.

Friday 29th May 2020

Total UK Deaths: 324 taking the total to 38,161

Confirmed Cases: 271,222

- Fraud victims have lost more than £4.6m to coronavirus-related scams during lockdown, according to figures released by Actionfraud, the UK's online centre for reporting fraud and cybercrime. Scams such as fake goods sold online, bogus cold calls, non-existent pension plans have all resulted in the loss of money.
- South Korea has been forced to close hundreds of schools, museums and art galleries, due to a fresh spike in coronavirus cases. The past 3 days have seen 177 new COVID-19 infections reported.
- Chancellor Rishi Sunak has unveiled new plans which will see employers beginning to pay towards the salaries of workers on the governments furlough scheme. The main changes will begin in August with the government continuing to pay 80% of salaries with a cap at £2,500, but employers must start paying National Insurance and pension contributions. In September the cap will reduce to £2,190 with the government paying 70%. The employer must then pay the extra 10% as well as contributions. In October that will become 60% with a cap at £1,875. The employer must then pay the 20% and the contributions. However, there are fears the changes may lead to a wave of redundancies as the country heads into a recession.
- Contact tracers on the governments new track and trace scheme are still experiencing technical difficulties on the plans second day of operation. Already there is talk of

people giving up on the scheme, as issues such as logging in and being paid cause great unrest.

So, we are done, at least for now. Today we completed our last shift as Team A. It was quite a strange feeling knowing the next time I am at the kennels it will be back to something like normal, with more people in.

I think the best way to describe the feeling is to imagine being sent on a training course which you don't really want to go on. For the duration of the course you have to work in a very small team. They are the only people you will interact with, and over time you will share so many experiences, good and bad. Then it comes to an end and the way of life which you have come accustomed too goes back to how it was before and the pressures of your daily job. In such time you get to know people better than you did at the start of it all, you build relationships and share the magic of what you have achieved in the short time you have been thrown together, as well as the downers.

Obviously, it is slightly different for us as we will all continue to work alongside each other on some days, but the realisation of this period in the history of the charity coming to an end makes us all a little sad I think.

When Boris Johnson announced we were going into lockdown, the thought of what we were going to have to do filled me with dread. I wasn't sure it would be possible to maintain the standard of care which the dogs were already receiving, but the truth is I think having to adapt has made things even better. We have had to change things, especially the way we operate when cleaning, but by using the outdoor kennels we should have so much more time once the volunteers begin to come back.

I feel as if I have connected with every single one of our very special dogs again. So many of them I rarely walked before lockdown because volunteers were in, but during these weeks I have handled all the dogs and been able to assess where I believe they are. I have seen good traits, bad manners, behavioural issues and improvements. I have been able to correct some of the issues and put plans in place to take things forward. I have been reintroduced to some fantastic characters, with dogs such as Casper, Max and Benji all making such fantastic progress. I probably wouldn't have had such hands on with any of them if things hadn't been the way they have. Working the way we have has reminded me it was me who gave them this second chance, it should be me who guides my team towards taking their lives further.

I have been able to identify strengths, and weaknesses, in my team members and will look to work with both sets of skills from now on in. Working together and improving each other will all help the dogs experience a more fulfilled existence. I believe we will be a better organisation for going through this which in turn can only be better for the dogs.

Rachel hit the nail on the head this afternoon when she said she felt sad knowing the next shift she does will mean she will have to share all these wonderful dogs with others. We have all grown so close to the animals we serve. I think the sadness we may never have such direct and exclusive contact sums up the feeling today.

Pride we have gotten through this, and gained so much, sadness it has come to an end and will probably never be like this again, but also gratitude we have been able to spend so much valuable time and so many special moments with these amazing dogs. Times which I for one, will not forget.

Day Sixty Eight.

Saturday 30th May 2020

Total UK Deaths: 215 taking the total to 38,376

Confirmed Cases: 272,826

- Three scientists from the Scientific Advisory Group for Emergencies (SAGE) have warned that the Government's plan to ease lockdown restrictions from Monday are too soon and it will lead to a rise in infection rates. The announcement which says from Monday, people will be able to meet up with groups from up to six households outside as long as social distancing is observed, has come just as the country enjoys a weekend of high temperatures and glorious sunshine.
- A gang of monkeys in India have "grabbed and fled" with coronavirus infected blood samples after attacking a laboratory technician. Now there are fears the monkeys may have carried the samples into residential areas or even spilled the samples. Doctor S.K Garg, a top official at the college where the samples were taken from, said it was unknown whether the monkeys could contract coronavirus by coming into contact with the infected blood.

I have been taking advantage of the aforementioned glorious weather to try and work on the story which I have called 'Home' and is to appear in Dominic Hodgson's eBook. I decided to try and concentrate on just one issue, with separation anxiety being told from the dog's point of view. Here is the first finished draft.

Home.

It is all so strange here. I have no idea what I am supposed to do, even more importantly I have no idea what I shouldn't be doing. One thing I do know though, is that I love it.

Everyone is so excitable and seem pleased that I am here, the children love it when we play. Dad likes to take me out on the concrete before we hit the green grass of what he calls "the park." Whilst Mam cuddles me up on the comfy seat once the children go upstairs. She strokes the top of my head, whilst she stares at the strange box in the corner of the room that has all the moving pictures on it.

The boy is the most fun, he wants to run and scream, then run and scream, then run and scream some more. Of course, I want to join in, who wouldn't? I run and bark, chase and bark, then run some more. I don't care if I knock plant pots over, I don't even see the girl as I zoom around the garden following the high pitched cries of joy. It wasn't my intention to knock her over.

I got wrong then, it made me feel bad. I was only trying to make the children happy. How was I to know that there were rules and places I was not allowed to go. The last time I was anywhere like a place like this, I was kicked every time I lifted my head off the makeshift bed of old newspapers and cigarette boxes that shared the space in the garage with me. My world amounted to nothing else but that dirty place.

I took those beatings because I knew nothing else. I took them because, despite the pain and the blood, I loved him. I had no one else.

I love my new family more though. They don't treat me like that and being with them is so much fun. I miss them when they go, Its awful. I hate being on my own, it makes me feel afraid and vulnerable. I have spent so much time on my own already.

It is easy to tell the days that I am going to be left alone. That strange screech of a noise happens earlier than other days, instantly I run to the bottom of the stairs, as I am not allowed up them, I have already learnt that lesson. I wait to see who will come down first, knowing that the hustle and bustle of everybody getting up together and wanting to be in the one room at the same time will happen at any second. That is when the arguments start, also when I retreat into my bed under the stairs and pretend that I am asleep. I don't want to get involved in that. I cannot help but shake at the sound of the shouting. It reminds me of where I used to live.

We all have breakfast together, although they sit at the big bench and my food is put in the far corner near the back door. I keep glancing over my shoulder to make sure that they are all still there, counting them one by one, but I enjoy my food so much. Where I used to live sometimes, I'd go days without getting anything to eat. It's all so new getting it at the same time every day, now it is something that I look forward to. "He needs Routine." Mam always says.

The boy likes his cereal, he adores to look for the gift at the bottom of the box. The girl has her headphones on most of the time, that sometimes leads to another argument. They are both dressed in the same colours, on the chest of their jumpers is the same symbol, the cloth around their necks has the same stripy pattern.

The hustle and bustle begin again, as Dad picks up his brief case and his car keys. He gives them all a kiss on their cheeks, Mam first, then boy, then girl who tries her best to avoid the contact. Then the sound of the car engine.

Mam hurries around and gets the children to put their coats on, then she too picks up her car keys. I hear the creak as the front door closes, then the sound of the smaller engine disappearing off the drive.

They are gone.

The sound of the birds, busy with their own morning outside, buses passing by the bottom of the street, the roar of an aeroplane as it flies over head, then the house descends into the blanket of loneliness. I walk to my bed from the passage where I watched them all leave one by one and let out a little sigh as I slump onto the red pillow with little grey bones on it. I hate being on my own.

The man in the red van comes to the door. I don't know what he wants, but he comes every day at about the same time. As soon as I hear the engine come down the street I am up out of my bed and racing to the front door. Waiting for him to attack, starting to pace the passage, then as he gets to next door I start to circle frantically, yelping with excitement at the thought of seeing him off.

He is here, I can hear him open the gate. His footsteps get louder as he gets nearer my front door. I begin to bark, the pitch getting higher the closer he gets, then I lunge as he pushes his weapons through the door. I shred them all, the brown ones and the white ones. The ones I miss coming through the letter box, I destroy as they hit the floor. I don't realise that I have caught more in my mouth than the letters, so I don't stop. Little multi coloured bits of cloth from the rug that lies on the wooden floor, gets stuck in between my teeth, but I just keep on ripping everything up that I can. I am beyond control; this is more than just a game for me, it is a war against this intruder.

Very quickly the man with the red van knows this is a battle he cannot win and makes his way back down the path. It is only when I hear the sound of the gate click shut and his footsteps disappear down the street to intrude somebody else's garden, that I come out of my frenzy.

It has only been seconds, but the carnage is there for the humans to see when they return. Nobody will get into this house without them being here when I am in charge.

Bits of paper, rags of cloth and splatters of my spit decorate the hallway as I return to the sanctuary of my bed under the stairs. Exhausted but proud as punch of my achievements, I drift off to sleep. I cannot wait to see how pleased they are to see what I have done when they come home.

Mam gets home first, with the children. I hear the car on the drive and rush out of my bed to the door once more. Unlike before though, I am excited and happy to see them, my family has come home, I have successfully protected the house. I stand just out of reach of the door for when it opens, feet buried in shreds from my previous venture to the door, my tail wagging as ferociously as my ripping had been earlier.

The look on Mam's face as she walks in is not what I expect at all. She stands there for just a few seconds, then bursts into tears. The children rush in after her, curious at what has made their mother upset. The horror on their faces is quickly replaced by a *look that screams "get me out of here." Then they run past her and me, the thud of their feet ringing in my ears as they make their escape up the stairs to the safety of their bedrooms, two doors bang closed making me jump.*

Mam grabs me by the collar and drags me outside into the back garden. "You can stay there till Dad comes home and sees what you have done." I can only just make out the word 'done' over the slam of the back door.

When Dad gets home, I hear them shouting at each other. Then Mam storms upstairs like the children did and another door slam's shut. He doesn't speak to me, the only time I see him is when he slides a bowl of my tea out from around the door into the garden. He says nothing, he just delivers my food. Eventually when it begins to get dark, he lets me back into the house. He says nothing once more, shows me to my bed and then mounts the stairs, switching the lights off as he goes.

The sun begins to rise just as I hear the screech from above. I have forgotten about what had happened yesterday, I am just excited to see them all.

One by one they descend. Mam and Dad first, neither speak to me. Then the boy, he gives me a hug and tells me he loves me, until Mam sees him and gives him a stare that means "come and get your breakfast or else." The girl comes down last, she doesn't speak to me either, she is too busy on her phone as normal, but she pats me on the head to let me know that she knows I am there.

They go through the same routine as yesterday, only as they leave the boy decides that it is too warm for his jacket just before he goes through the door.

"Come on." Says Mam as she turns the ignition and the engine roars into life. *"We'll be late."*

"Coming." The boy says and he throws his coat onto the floor, right onto what remains of the expensive rug I half devoured yesterday.

I retreat to my bed, but my eyes quickly spring open when I hear the red van trundle down the street. He is back.

I go through the same routine as yesterday, only this time I don't realise that the quarry in my mouth is the boys coat. I rag it up and down, tearing it more and more every time I see white stuffing float out like the clouds in the sky. The buzz is immense, like nothing I have felt before. The more I shake my head, the more white fills the room. I hear the tears but don't associate it with what I am doing. I am so enthralled I don't even hear the postman leave. Long after he is gone, I continue my trail of destruction.

The small pile of shoes at the bottom of the stairs are next. I throw them into the air one by one, chewing at the pieces of string that hang from the fronts of them. Then the carpet on the bottom stair next to where they are kept grabs my attention.
I pull at the corner next to the wall and a whole strip of it comes up in my mouth. I keep pulling and more becomes mine, the first step then the second, then the third.

After pulling up the carpet from six stairs, the wooden spindles that hold up the bannister grab my attention. Sinking my teeth into the dark mahogany wood, a rush of excitement reverberates through my body as I see the marks I have left. The family will love my decorations when they come home. So, I continue to *chew, working my way nearly halfway up the staircase, until eventually I need a drink and a lie down.*

Reflecting on my mornings work from my bed, the feeling of satisfaction begins to fade away, replaced by anxiety as I remember the reaction of Mam and the consequences of last night. I shouldn't have done what I have done this morning, I will be punished again for sure. I just love them so much and miss them when they are not around. I hate being on my own, I am frightened that they won't come back to me, and I will become forgotten again.

My life up to this point has not been very enjoyable, I have never belonged anywhere, for the first time now I have a family of my own, I shouldn't have repaid them by doing what I have just done.

I lie in my bed for the rest of the day, shaking at the realisation of my actions and fear at the thought of facing the consequences. People pass the front window, but I don't move. I stay silent with my chin flat on the floor.

When the laughing and chattering school children pass, I don't see them off like I usually do, I keep in my den under the stairs and don't move.

Then I hear Mam's car pull onto the drive, the sound of three car doors opening and closing with a bang. Footsteps and then the key turns in the lock. I begin to shake even more; I am so frightened I urinate where I am lying. I hear the creak of the rusty door hinge Dad keeps promising to fix. The children are arguing with each other as they always seem to do when they come back from school. Then I hear shatter of a wine bottle as shopping bags fall to the ground and nestle in the remains of the boy's coat and the rug.

The children stop their confrontation.

The entire world falls into a deafening silence.

Day Sixty Nine.

Sunday 31st May 2020

Total UK Deaths: 113 taking the total to 38,489

Confirmed Cases: 274,762

- The latest figures from the Office for National Statistics announce the death toll from this pandemic could be even higher than the numbers which we are given on a daily basis. The figure from yesterday of 38,376 deaths are those registered after a positive test for COVID-19. However, the figure which mentions COVID-19 on the death certificate is 45,231. The ONS also reveal the number of deaths over and above the usual for this time of year is 59,297.
- Foreign Secretary Dominic Raab say's "we can't just stay in lockdown forever." He also says "steady progress" has been made in bringing down the transmission rate of coronavirus but adds "we are at a precarious moment. We must monitor it very carefully."
- The latest relaxation of lockdown rules will allow 2.2 million at-risk people who have been shielding in their homes since lockdown began to go outdoors with members of their household. Boris Johnson also announced those who live alone can meet outside with one other person from another household. The move faces another backlash from leading scientists, who claim the Government is moving too fast, whilst Labour leader Sir Keir Starmer has accused the Prime Minister of making difficult decisions riskier.
- Hundreds of revellers in east London have once again defied lockdown measures and gathered at an illegal party in Detmold Road, Clapton. Police used a helicopter to disperse the crowds, including a DJ.

- As the day progresses, I am left in absolute shock at the scenes from London, as hundreds gather in spots such as Trafalgar Square to continue on the protests which have ripped through America after the killing of unarmed black man George Floyd. Video footage of the protests go viral on all social media as well as news stations, with no evidence of social distancing present in any of them. Some of the crowds are wearing facemasks, but other than that, there is no thoughts for others or themselves. Everything which has been achieved in the last seventy days could have just been undone in one afternoon.

As we head towards tomorrow and all the changes it will bring, today I have the feeling of reflection and nerves I remember getting at the end of the school summer holidays. Since all this began on the dark night of Monday 23rd March, we have all been through so much and learnt a great deal along the way, as individuals, a charity and a society.

I have seen both the good and bad side of living on my own, as well as feeling the pain of missing others who I hold dear to my heart. I have felt safe in my home tucked away in the rural countryside and away from people, but also worried as lockdown regulations have been eased and the pedestrian traffic past my front door has increased.

Through the loses of Sheba and then Oscar, I have had to face the intrusive act of death in two very different ways. The drawn out version of doing all you can to avoid it, the hope and the resignation, but the outcome being the same as the sudden shock of the end just presenting itself out of the blue when you least expect it. Both are as equally painful and neither make it any easier. I miss them both every day.

I have witnessed great frustration from the people who have been unable to come to see the dogs which they love, but also a wonderful understanding of why it was the case. The reactions to changes have given me an insight into how peoples mind's work. I have learnt a lot about my team, not least the grit and determination to succeed even in the most difficult of circumstances. I am very proud of the way the charity has adapted and evolved, it is through such devotion we have survived this, we live to fight another day.

Tomorrow, as a country, we all go into uncertain and dangerous ground together. Nobody knows if it is the right thing to do or whether we are setting ourselves up for one almighty fall. I know my feelings on the subject, but it is the uncertainty across the board from the people at the top making the decisions, to the scientists whose research is advising against doing too much too soon, which is driving such fear.

I am excited at the days which I have scheduled into my own personal agenda, all of which I believe will hopefully benefit the dogs in the long run.

My first practical day is Tuesday. Already I have Merlin booked in for X Rays with Emily to see if we can get to the bottom of his limp. My fear of osteosarcoma is still there, but at least this way we will know for sure and then we will be able to take the appropriate action in terms of how he goes forward. Making the appointment itself is a huge move, as it seems so long ago since I originally mentioned the plan to get him checked over earlier in this book.

The vets are still not open to the public in terms of being able to go indoors, so whilst I wait for his results, I intend to put the time to good use. Accompanying me in the van will be Dande and Casper, two boys who will have some time away from kennel life for different reasons.

Dande, as I have already mentioned, is the little Romanian import we got from the vets just before lockdown. He was booked in to be destroyed because his behaviour had become difficult to manage. He is only two years old.

Having been with us for over three months now, we still haven't seen anything which would indicate he couldn't be placed in an experienced home. Hopefully a trip into the outside world will help assess him a little more closely and allow me to begin the process of finding him a place.

I've already told you Casper's story. Such a complex little character who is so set in his ways. Sometimes at the kennels he refuses to walk for volunteers, he simply puts the breaks on or pulls the other way. He doesn't do that for me though, so maybe he just thinks he can get away with it, I really don't know.

I thought taking him away from the comfort of his daily routine and the familiarity of where he goes, might give him something else to think about. It is so easy to pigeonhole a dog from the behaviour which we see every day in kennels, decisions on whether they can be rehomed or not are often made on such observations. I am hoping days such as this Tuesday will broaden our perspective and give the dogs even more of a chance.

So, this is the end of life as I have come to know since that monumental day in March. The routine of three days at the kennels and three at home will be no more. The trips to the Co-op in the quaint little village of Rothbury, where I ventured out for the first time and understood even in the most remote places, we were fighting against a silent killer, will not happen again. All of it to be consigned into my own memories which will fade over time but live on forever in this book.

The daily concentration of digesting the worldwide news and the charity's events, then producing them into the words which you have just read, will be no more. The loneliness and solitude of being a rescue in lockdown will now be nothing more than the words you have just read. Some you will have identified with, others you will have used your imagination to understand. I hope either way they have given you a clear picture of what it has been like.

Whilst I am pleased we are moving back to normality and I will be able to see my loved ones, I feel sad too. I am going to miss the simplicity of life and routine, and the feeling of safety which has come with it.

Day Seventy.

Monday 1st June 2020

Total UK Deaths: To be confirmed…

Confirmed Cases: To be confirmed…

7.49am. I have just pulled up at the kennels. The sky is blue, and the sun is shining so bright. No sign of black clouds and no need for rainbows today. This morning is a celebration of the start of a new month, and also a new start completely for how we work. The dark months of lockdown are now over, the rainbow is stretched out over the sky, the recovery starts today.

The first volunteer pulls into the farmyard, just as I begin to unlock the padlock to the kennels front door. Waves are exchanged for the first time in seventy days. I can see excitement on the face of the person behind the wheel. For them this is like being allowed out to play after months of being grounded by your parents. Freedom, liberation, an opportunity to see so many loved ones which they have been starved the opportunity to do so. As one set of tyres disappear down the track to the car park around the back, I hear the sound of the next ones disturbing the stones which make up the farmyard. I have already gone inside by the time the vehicle passes the door.

This is the first day of a new beginning, a new dawn and a new chapter. A fresh start in every sense of the word. Everything we have worked so hard to protect is now vulnerable once more, but also everything we have strived to improve gains the benefit from here on in.

Wish us luck.

Reading through those dark days, as I do a number of times to edit, has reminded me just how worrying and depressing those days during lockdown were. I am proud we managed to cope and survive and, I am still amazed at the fantastic support we got from our supporters. We honestly couldn't have done it without you, the charity would simply be no longer here.

Writing this now, halfway through September the fear and worry is still as strong for me. As summertime moves away from these shores and autumn begins to take hold, it looks as if we are facing the second wave which so many predicted during the 70 days my book covers. Total lockdown has been replaced by individual area lockdowns, the restrictions which were eased so people could socialise are slowly creeping back into full force. I am concerned where all this is heading.

This morning I received an email from a reliable source claiming there will be a government announcement tomorrow which will see Northumberland go into some form of local lockdown. We will be back to square one and going through all of this again.

The changes we made during the original lockdown are still in force today and, we are all still seeing the benefits. Dogs are out three times most days, incredible when you consider we were worrying if we would be able to make the two trips out, other enrichment plans such as days away are in place.

My practical days have been a huge success and have helped me learn so much about the dogs as individuals in the outside world, rather than seeing them in the kennel environment. So much so, four have now moved on into homes which probably wouldn't have happened if we hadn't shared such valuable time together.

Like all my books, there has been no professional help with any element of the project. Everything you have read has been put together in the spirit of a true indie writer, the cover is photographs taken by me and then edited, it is myself who has published the final product.

There will be mistakes, I know there are. Some you will spot, some you will not, but I have tried my best to give a true and honest account of a time I thought the world might end. I hope it has been good enough for you to at least enjoy reading it.

I would however, like to thank the following people, all of which played a part in getting SHAK through this.

The staff and extra volunteers who came in to make the teams up to a four. Without the commitment, personal sacrifice and hard work of these people it simply would not have happened.

To Joan and Jon for taking the increased pressure of being a Trustee so well, and to Sandra for her role as an advisor and a soundboard.

To the landlords of various properties connected to the charity for being understanding about the financial aspect all of this has had on the day to day survival.

To everyone who donated to help us get through. Whether it be financial or physical in terms of things we needed. Once again amazing support we couldn't have done without.

To the members of the media who got behind us and promoted the plight we were facing. Exposure which really helped beyond belief.

To the volunteers who understood and lived with the frustration of not being able to come in, and for their loyalty in returning when they could.

Thanks to Sky News and BBC News for the media stories and daily figures.

To my Dad Ian who took the time to read through this and try and point out as many mistakes as he could find. His first time ever as a proof-reader, I'm sure it won't be his last.

To Michael Robinson who volunteers his expertise and patience in designing all the SHAK stationery and calendars. This time he helped pull the technical side of the covers together. Just as I was tearing the little bit of hair I have left out.

Lastly to the dogs in our care who really did take everything in their stride and adapted to the situation so well. I am proud of each and everyone of them and will continue to do everything I can to make their lives fuller and more content.

I hope through reading what you just have, you can associate with some of the feelings and situations I found myself in, I hope the picture I have painted reflects what living in lockdown was like, not only for a rescue but for each and every one of us.

Whilst I doubt it will be the case, I hope we never have to go through it again.

Keep safe.

www.shak.org.uk

Other books available by the author:

It's A Dog's Life

Only Human

The Castle

All available at www.stephenwylie.com